Julia for Scientific Computing

Julia in Production: A Data Science Journey

Alexander Clifton

Published by Northwood Lore Books, 2024.

JULIA FOR SCIENTIFIC COMPUTING

First edition. November 18, 2024.

ISBN: 979-8230074601

Written by Alexander Clifton.

Table of Contents

Chapter 1: Introduction to Julia for Data Scientists

Welcome to the exciting world of Julia programming for data science! As we embark on this journey together, it's essential to understand why Julia has emerged as a powerful alternative to traditional data science languages like Python and R. In this chapter, we'll explore the fundamental reasons behind Julia's growing popularity and why it might be the perfect choice for your next data science project.

Julia was created in 2012 by Jeff Bezanson, Stefan Karpinski, Viral Shah, and Alan Edelman at MIT. Their vision was to develop a high-level programming language that could match the ease of use of Python and R while delivering the performance of lower-level languages like C and Fortran. This ambitious goal has been largely achieved, making Julia particularly attractive for data scientists who work with large-scale computations and complex numerical algorithms.

One of the most compelling features of Julia is its solution to what's known as the "two-language problem." Traditionally, data scientists would prototype their ideas in a high-level language like Python or R, but when performance became critical, they would need to rewrite their code in a faster language like C++ or Fortran. This process is time-consuming, error-prone, and requires maintaining code in multiple languages. Julia eliminates this problem by providing both rapid development capabilities and excellent performance in a single language.

The performance advantages of Julia stem from several key design decisions. First, Julia is a just-in-time (JIT) compiled language, which means that code is compiled to machine code right before execution. This approach combines the interactive development experience of interpreted languages with the performance benefits of compiled languages. Second, Julia's type system is designed to be both flexible and performant, allowing developers to write generic code that can be specialized for different types at runtime. This feature, combined with multiple dispatch (which we'll explore in detail in Chapter 6), enables Julia to generate highly optimized machine code for specific input types.

For data scientists coming from Python or R, Julia offers many familiar concepts while introducing powerful new capabilities. The language supports a wide range of programming paradigms, including functional, object-oriented, and metaprogramming approaches. This flexibility allows developers to choose the most appropriate style for their specific needs while maintaining code readability and maintainability.

The Julia ecosystem has matured significantly since its inception. The package manager, Pkg, provides a robust system for managing dependencies and project environments. The growing collection of packages covers everything from data manipulation (DataFrames.jl) to machine learning (MLJ.jl) and deep learning (Flux.jl). Many of these packages are designed with performance in mind and take full advantage of Julia's unique features.

One of Julia's standout features is its built-in support for parallel and distributed computing. While languages like Python often require additional frameworks or complex setup procedures for parallel execution, Julia makes it straightforward to parallelize code across multiple cores or machines. This capability is particularly valuable for data scientists working with large datasets or computationally intensive algorithms.

The integration capabilities of Julia are another significant advantage. Through packages like PyCall.jl and RCall.jl, Julia can seamlessly interact with Python and R code, allowing data scientists to leverage existing libraries while gradually transitioning their workflows to Julia. This interoperability means you can adopt Julia incrementally, starting with performance-critical components while maintaining access to the rich ecosystems of Python and R.

As we progress through this book, you'll discover that Julia excels in numerous areas crucial to production data science. Its strong type system and multiple dispatch capabilities enable the creation of robust, reusable code. The built-in package development tools and testing frameworks facilitate the creation of production-ready applications. The language's support for GPU computing through CUDA.jl opens up possibilities for accelerating machine learning workloads.

However, it's important to acknowledge that transitioning to Julia does come with some challenges. The language is relatively young compared to Python and R, which means the ecosystem, while growing rapidly, may not yet have direct equivalents for all specialized libraries available in other languages. The learning curve can be steeper, particularly when it comes to understanding concepts like multiple dispatch and type systems. Additionally, compilation times can sometimes be longer than desired, although this is often offset by faster execution times.

Throughout this book, we'll address these challenges head-on and provide practical strategies for overcoming them. You'll learn how to structure your code for optimal performance, how to leverage Julia's unique features effectively, and how to build and deploy production-ready data science applications.

The journey from development to production deployment involves many considerations beyond just writing efficient code. We'll explore best practices for testing, continuous integration, containerization, and deployment. You'll learn how to monitor and maintain Julia applications in production environments, handle errors gracefully, and scale your applications as needed.

Real-world case studies will demonstrate how organizations are using Julia to solve complex problems in various domains, from financial analytics to bioinformatics. These examples will provide concrete insights into how Julia can be applied effectively in production settings and the benefits it can bring to your data science workflows.

As we conclude this introduction, it's worth emphasizing that Julia represents more than just another programming language; it represents a fundamental shift in how we approach scientific computing and data science. By providing a single language that excels at both rapid prototyping and high-performance computing, Julia enables data scientists to focus more on solving problems and less on technical implementation details.

In the following chapters, we'll dive deep into the practical aspects of using Julia for data science, starting with setting up your development environment and gradually progressing to advanced topics in production deployment. Whether you're a Python developer looking to improve performance, an R user seeking more robust tools for large-scale computing, or simply curious about what Julia has to offer, this book will guide you through the process of becoming proficient in Julia for production data science.

Remember that the transition to Julia doesn't have to be all-or-nothing. You can start small, perhaps by implementing performance-critical components in Julia while maintaining the rest of your workflow in your current language. As you become more comfortable with Julia and discover its benefits firsthand, you can gradually expand its use in your projects. The key is to approach the transition strategically, focusing on areas where Julia's strengths can provide the most significant benefits to your specific use case.

Chapter 2: Setting Up Your Julia Development Environment

Chapter 2: Setting Up Your Julia Development Environment

Setting up a robust development environment is crucial for productive work with Julia. In this chapter, we'll walk through the essential steps and best practices for creating an environment that supports both learning and production development. We'll cover everything from basic installation to advanced tooling configuration.

The first step in your Julia journey is installing the language itself. Julia can be downloaded from the official website (julialang.org), which provides installers for Windows, macOS, and Linux. It's recommended to use the latest stable version unless you have specific requirements for an older release. The installation process is straightforward: download the appropriate installer for your operating system and follow the standard installation steps. On Unix-based systems, you might prefer to use package managers like apt or brew, though the direct download from the official website often provides the most up-to-date version.

Once Julia is installed, you'll want to verify the installation by opening a terminal and typing "julia". This should launch the Julia REPL (Read-Eval-Print Loop), which provides an interactive environment for testing code and managing packages. The REPL is more than just a simple command prompt; it offers several powerful modes accessed by different characters. The default mode (>) is for executing Julia code, while the package mode (]) is used for managing packages, the shell mode (;) provides access to system commands, and the help mode (?) offers documentation.

For serious development work, you'll need a proper Integrated Development Environment (IDE) or text editor. Visual Studio Code (VS Code) with the Julia extension has emerged as the de facto standard IDE for Julia development. The Julia extension provides features like syntax highlighting, code completion, inline documentation, plot pane integration, and debugging capabilities. To set up VS Code for Julia development, install VS Code first, then add the Julia extension from the marketplace. The extension will automatically detect your Julia installation and configure itself accordingly.

Another popular option is Jupyter notebooks, which are excellent for exploratory data analysis and creating reproducible research documents. Julia integrates seamlessly with Jupyter through the IJulia package. To set up Jupyter with Julia support, first launch Julia's package mode by typing "]" in the REPL, then run "add IJulia". This will install both IJulia and, if necessary, Jupyter itself. Once installed, you can start a Jupyter notebook server with Julia support by running "using IJulia" followed by "notebook()" in the Julia REPL.

Environment management is a critical aspect of Julia development, particularly for production applications. Julia's built-in package manager provides robust support for project-specific environments, similar to Python's virtual environments. To create a new project, navigate to your desired directory in the REPL's package mode and run "generate ProjectName". This creates a new project with its own Project.toml and Manifest.toml files, which track dependencies and their versions.

The Project.toml file specifies direct dependencies and their version constraints, while Manifest.toml records the exact versions of all packages (including transitive dependencies) used in your project. This system ensures reproducibility across different machines and environments. When sharing your code, you typically version control the Project.toml file but not the Manifest.toml, unless exact package versions are critical for your application.

For production environments, it's important to set up proper logging and debugging tools. Julia's built-in Logging standard library provides basic logging functionality, but you might want to consider additional packages like LoggingExtras.jl for more advanced features. For debugging, the Debugger.jl package offers a powerful interactive debugger that can be used both from the REPL and VS Code.

Performance profiling is another essential aspect of the development environment. Julia includes a built-in profiler accessed through the Profile module, but you might want to install additional tools like ProfileView.jl for visualization or BenchmarkTools.jl for detailed performance benchmarking. These tools are invaluable when optimizing code for production use.

When working with data science projects, you'll want to set up common packages that you'll use frequently. A typical data science stack might include DataFrames.jl for tabular data manipulation, Plots.jl for visualization, Statistics for basic statistical functions, and MLJ.jl for machine learning. You can create a template environment with these packages and reuse it across projects.

Git integration is crucial for version control. While Git itself is language-agnostic, there are some Julia-specific considerations. Create a .gitignore file that excludes Manifest.toml (unless needed), .ipynb_checkpoints/ for Jupyter notebooks, and any large data files. Consider using Git LFS (Large File Storage) for managing large datasets or model files.

For continuous integration and testing, Julia works well with common CI platforms like GitHub Actions, GitLab CI, or Jenkins. You'll want to set up automated testing using Julia's built-in Test module and possibly additional testing packages like SafeTestsets.jl for more structured testing. Create a .github/workflows directory in your project and set up workflow files for automated testing and deployment.

Docker containerization is increasingly important for production deployments. Create a Dockerfile that includes Julia and your project dependencies. The official Julia Docker images provide a good starting point. Consider multi-stage builds to keep the final image size small while maintaining development capabilities in your build environment.

Security considerations should be addressed early in your development setup. Use Julia's built-in SSL/TLS support for secure communications, and consider setting up GPG signing for your Git commits. When working with sensitive data, ensure your development environment is properly isolated and secured.

Finally, set up proper documentation tools. Julia's built-in documentation system, accessed through Documenter.jl, allows you to create comprehensive documentation directly from your source code. Configure automatic documentation deployment through GitHub Pages or similar services.

Remember to regularly update your Julia installation and packages, but do so carefully in production environments. Use package version pinning in Project.toml to maintain stability, and test thoroughly after any updates. Consider setting up a local package server or mirror for air-gapped environments or to ensure package availability.

Your development environment should also include tools for monitoring system resources. While Julia's garbage collector handles memory management automatically, tools like SystemMonitor.jl can help you track resource usage during development and testing.

By following these setup guidelines, you'll create a robust development environment that supports both learning and production work with Julia. In the next chapter, we'll build on this foundation as we explore Julia's syntax and how it compares to Python and R.

Chapter 3: Julia Syntax for Python and R Users

Chapter 3 focuses on helping Python and R users transition to Julia by understanding its syntax differences and similarities. Let's dive into the key aspects of Julia's syntax that will feel both familiar and novel to those coming from these popular data science languages.

For Python users, Julia's syntax will feel immediately familiar in many ways. Like Python, Julia uses indentation to enhance code readability, though unlike Python, indentation is not syntactically significant. Code blocks in Julia are explicitly terminated with the end keyword, similar to Ruby or MATLAB. This explicit termination makes the code structure clear and helps prevent indentation related errors that can plague Python code.

One of the most noticeable differences for Python users is Julia's array indexing. While Python uses zero based indexing, Julia, like R, uses one based indexing. This means that the first element of an array is accessed with index 1 rather than 0. For example, if we have an array arr, we access its first element with arr[1] in Julia, not arr[0] as in Python. This can take some getting used to, but it aligns well with mathematical notation and makes certain algorithms more intuitive to implement.

Function definitions in Julia offer multiple styles that will feel comfortable to both Python and R users. The most common way to define a function uses the function keyword followed by the function name and parameters, similar to Python's def keyword. However, Julia also supports a more concise single line function definition style that resembles mathematical notation or R's arrow syntax. For example, you can write f(x) = x^2 instead of the more verbose function f(x) return x^2 end.

Variable assignment in Julia follows similar conventions to Python and R, using the = operator. However, Julia distinguishes between assignment (=) and equality testing (==) more strictly than R does. This helps prevent a common source of bugs in R code where assignment and comparison can sometimes be confused. Julia also supports multiple assignment in a single line, similar to Python's tuple unpacking: x, y = 1, 2 is valid Julia code.

For R users, Julia's vectorization capabilities will feel natural. Like R, Julia supports element wise operations on arrays using standard mathematical operators. However, Julia takes this a step further with its dot syntax for vectorizing any function. For example, if f is a function, f.(array) applies f to each element of array. This is more consistent and powerful than R's vectorization approaches, while being more explicit than Python's numpy vectorization.

String manipulation in Julia combines familiar concepts from both Python and R. String literals can use either single or double quotes, like Python, and support similar escape sequences. Julia's string interpolation syntax uses $ to embed expressions within strings, which is more concise than Python's f strings or R's paste function. For example, "The result is $x" will interpolate the value of x directly into the string.

Control flow structures in Julia will be familiar to both Python and R users, but with some important differences. While if statements and for loops exist in all three languages, Julia's for loops are more flexible than Python's and more performant than R's. Julia supports multiple iterator variables in a single for loop naturally: for (i, j) in zip(1:10, 11:20). The break and continue statements work as expected from Python.

Julia's comprehension syntax closely resembles Python's list comprehensions, making it easy for Python users to transition. However, Julia's comprehensions are more powerful, supporting multiple input variables and multiple conditions. For example, [i+j for i in 1:3, j in 1:3 if i != j] creates a matrix comprehension with a condition, something that would require more verbose code in Python.

Exception handling in Julia uses try/catch blocks similar to Python, but with some syntactic differences. The finally clause works the same way, ensuring code execution regardless of whether an exception occurred. Julia's error types are organized in a clear hierarchy, making it easy to catch specific types of errors while letting others propagate.

One aspect that might surprise both Python and R users is Julia's macro system, denoted by the @ symbol. Macros are a powerful metaprogramming feature that allows code transformation at parse time. While initially unfamiliar, macros enable powerful abstractions and are commonly used in Julia packages. For example, @time measures execution time, similar to Python's timeit or R's system.time.

Broadcasting in Julia deserves special attention as it represents a more systematic approach to vectorization than either Python or R. The dot syntax (.) can be used to broadcast any function or operator over arrays of compatible shapes. This is more consistent than Python's numpy broadcasting rules and more powerful than R's vectorization.

Type annotations in Julia are optional but can be useful for code clarity and performance. Unlike Python's type hints, Julia's type annotations are actually used by the compiler to generate efficient code. The syntax is similar to Python's type hints but uses :: instead of :. For example, function f(x::Float64)::Float64 specifies that both the input and output should be 64 bit floating point numbers.

Julia's package management syntax will feel somewhat familiar to R users who have used devtools or remotes. The package mode in the REPL, accessed with], provides commands like add, remove, and update that work similarly to pip in Python or install.packages in R. However, Julia's package manager is more powerful, handling dependencies and environments more robustly than either Python's pip or R's package system.

Comments in Julia use the # symbol for single line comments, familiar to both Python and R users. Multiline comments use #= and =# delimiters, which might take some getting used to for users of either language. Documentation strings use """ triple quotes similar to Python, but are placed before the object being documented rather than after.

Regular expressions in Julia use similar syntax to Python and R but with some additional capabilities. The r"pattern" string prefix creates a regular expression, similar to Python's r strings. However, Julia's regex support includes some unique features like verbose regular expressions with embedded comments.

The concept of nothing in Julia serves a similar purpose to Python's None or R's NULL, but with some important differences. Julia's nothing is a singleton of type Nothing, and is used to indicate the absence of a value. However, Julia's type system handles nothing more consistently than Python's None or R's NULL, leading to fewer special cases in code.

Anonymous functions in Julia use a syntax that might be familiar to R users of the purrr package, with x -> x^2 being equivalent to Python's lambda x: x^2. However, Julia's anonymous functions are more powerful and can include multiple lines of code when needed.

Understanding these syntax differences and similarities is crucial for effectively transitioning to Julia from Python or R. While there may be an initial learning curve, Julia's syntax choices generally lead to more consistent and maintainable code once mastered. The next chapter will build on this foundation as we explore Julia's data structures and collections in detail.

Chapter 4: Basic Data Structures and Collections

Data structures and collections form the backbone of any programming language, and Julia provides a rich set of built-in options that combine performance with flexibility. In this chapter, we'll explore the fundamental data structures available in Julia and understand how to use them effectively in data science applications.

Arrays are perhaps the most important collection type in Julia, particularly for data science applications. Unlike Python's lists, Julia's arrays are designed for high performance numerical computing. They are homogeneous, meaning all elements must be of the same type, which allows for efficient memory layout and faster computations. Arrays can be created using square bracket syntax: simple_array = [1, 2, 3]. Julia supports multidimensional arrays natively, without requiring a separate package like NumPy. Creating a 2D array is as straightforward as using nested brackets or the matrix construction syntax: matrix = [1 2 3; 4 5 6].

One powerful feature of Julia's arrays is their ability to view and slice data without copying. When you create a view of an array using the view function or the @view macro, you're creating a reference to the original data rather than a copy. This is particularly important when working with large datasets where memory efficiency is crucial. For example, data_view = @view large_array[1:1000, :] creates a view of the first thousand rows of a matrix without allocating new memory.

Tuples in Julia serve a similar purpose to their Python counterparts but with some important differences. Julia has both regular tuples, created with parentheses like (1, 2, 3), and named tuples, which allow you to give names to each element: person = (name = "John", age = 30). Named tuples are particularly useful in data science applications where you want to maintain the relationship between values and their meanings while keeping the efficiency of a tuple structure.

Dictionaries in Julia, created using Dict(), function similarly to Python dictionaries or R named lists. They provide key value mappings with fast lookup times. Julia's dictionaries are type stable, meaning the types of keys and values are maintained consistently, leading to better performance. You can create a dictionary with various syntaxes: dict = Dict("a" => 1, "b" => 2) or dict = Dict(zip(keys, values)). Dictionaries are particularly useful for creating lookup tables or maintaining mappings between different data elements.

Sets in Julia represent collections of unique elements and are created using Set(). They support standard set operations like union, intersection, and difference with an elegant syntax. For example, union(set1, set2) combines two sets, while intersect(set1, set2) finds common elements. Sets are particularly useful in data science for finding unique values in data or performing set based operations on categorical variables.

Julia provides several specialized collection types that are particularly useful for data science applications. The Range type, created using the : operator or range function, represents sequences of values without actually storing all elements in memory. This is extremely memory efficient for large sequences. For example, 1:1000000 creates a range object that represents all integers from 1 to 1000000 without allocating memory for each number.

BitArrays are specialized arrays for boolean values that pack multiple boolean values into single bytes, making them memory efficient for logical operations. They're particularly useful in data science for boolean indexing and mask operations. Similarly, SparseArrays provide efficient storage for arrays with many zero elements, common in fields like natural language processing and network analysis.

One of Julia's unique features is its support for custom collection types through the AbstractArray interface. This allows you to create specialized array types that behave like regular arrays but with custom behavior. For example, you might create a custom array type that automatically logs access patterns or implements domain specific optimization.

Queue and deque (double ended queue) data structures are available through the DataStructures.jl package. These are essential for implementing algorithms that require FIFO (first in, first out) or LIFO (last in, first out) behavior. The package also provides other specialized collections like priority queues, which are useful in implementing certain algorithms.

CircularBuffers, also available through DataStructures.jl, are fixed size buffers that overwrite oldest elements when full. These are particularly useful in streaming data applications or when implementing sliding window computations on time series data.

Julia's strings are immutable sequences of Unicode characters, similar to Python 3 strings. However, Julia provides additional string types for different encodings and use cases. The SubString type, for example, allows efficient string slicing without copying data. This is particularly useful when processing large text datasets.

For working with missing data, Julia provides the missing value type, which is more sophisticated than Python's None or R's NA. The missing type properly propagates through calculations and supports three valued logic, making it ideal for handling real world datasets with incomplete information.

One of Julia's powerful features is its support for memory views through the reshape function and view operations. These allow you to work with data in different shapes without copying it, which is particularly useful when working with large datasets or implementing complex numerical algorithms.

When working with collections, Julia provides comprehensive iteration tools. The enumerate function combines an iterator with a counter, similar to Python. The zip function combines multiple iterators into a single iterator of tuples. These tools are essential for data processing tasks where you need to track indices or combine multiple data sources.

Julia's broadcast mechanism deserves special mention when discussing collections. Broadcasting allows you to apply functions element wise to arrays of different shapes, automatically expanding singleton dimensions as needed. This is more flexible and powerful than similar features in Python's NumPy or R's vectorization.

Understanding Julia's collection types and their performance characteristics is crucial for writing efficient data science code. While Python users might be tempted to use arrays like Python lists, and R users might reach for lists like R vectors, taking advantage of Julia's specialized collection types can lead to significant performance improvements and more maintainable code.

The next chapter will build on this foundation by exploring Julia's type system in detail, showing how these collection types fit into Julia's broader type hierarchy and how to use type information to write more efficient code.

Chapter 5: Julia's Type System Fundamentals

Julia's type system is one of its most distinctive features, setting it apart from dynamically typed languages like Python and R. Understanding the type system is crucial for writing efficient, maintainable code and fully leveraging Julia's multiple dispatch capabilities.

At its core, Julia uses a dynamic type system with static type inference. This means that while you don't need to declare types explicitly in most cases, the compiler can often determine the types of variables at compile time. This combination provides the flexibility of dynamic typing with the performance benefits of static typing.

Every value in Julia has a type, which you can check using the typeof function. Types themselves are also values and have the type Type. This metaclass system allows for powerful abstractions and generic programming patterns. For example, typeof(1) returns Int64, while typeof(Int64) returns DataType.

Julia's type system is hierarchical, with all types ultimately descending from the Any type. At the bottom of the hierarchy is Union{}, representing the empty type with no values. Between these extremes lies a rich tree of both abstract and concrete types. Abstract types serve as categories or interfaces and cannot be instantiated directly, while concrete types represent actual values that can be created and used in your code.

One of the fundamental concepts in Julia's type system is type stability. A function is type stable if the compiler can determine the return type based solely on the input types. Type stable code generally performs better because the compiler can generate optimized machine code. Consider a simple function: if your function sometimes returns an integer and sometimes a float depending on a runtime condition, it's type unstable and may perform poorly.

Primitive types in Julia are concrete types that represent basic building blocks like numbers. You can define your own primitive types using the primitive type keyword, though this is relatively rare in data science applications. More commonly, you'll work with built in primitives like Int64, Float64, and Bool.

Composite types, defined using the struct keyword, allow you to create custom data structures. These are similar to classes in object oriented languages but with some important differences. A basic composite type might look like this: struct Person name::String age::Int64 end. The ::Type syntax specifies type annotations, which are optional but can improve performance and code clarity.

Julia supports parametric types, allowing you to create types that take parameters. This is similar to generics in other languages. For example, Array{T,N} is a parametric type where T represents the element type and N represents the number of dimensions. You can create your own parametric types: struct DataContainer{T} data::T end.

Type unions, created using Union{Type1,Type2}, allow you to specify that a value can be one of several types. This is particularly useful when working with missing data, where you might use Union{Float64,Missing} to indicate that a value can be either a floating point number or missing.

Abstract types serve as interfaces or categories in Julia. You can define your own abstract types using the abstract type keyword. Abstract types form the backbone of Julia's type hierarchy and are crucial for multiple dispatch. When defining new types, you can specify their supertype using the <: operator: abstract type MyNumber <: Number end.

Type parameters can have constraints, limiting what types can be used as parameters. For instance, Array{T,N} where {T<:Number} restricts T to be a subtype of Number. These constraints help catch errors at compile time and can improve performance by allowing more specific code generation.

Mutable structs, defined using mutable struct, allow you to create objects whose fields can be modified after creation. While immutable structs (the default) are generally preferred for their performance benefits and thread safety, mutable structs are sometimes necessary for implementing certain algorithms or data structures.

Type conversion and promotion are handled elegantly in Julia. The convert function attempts to convert values to a specified type, while promotion rules determine how different types are automatically converted when used together in operations. You can define your own conversion and promotion rules for custom types.

Julia's type system includes support for singleton types, which are types that can have only one instance. These are useful for implementing certain design patterns and for dispatch. You can create singleton types using struct with no fields.

Type aliases, created using const Type2 = Type1, allow you to give alternative names to types. This is useful for creating more domain specific terminology or for shortening long type names. Type aliases are purely for convenience and don't create new types.

The type system includes support for diagonal types, where type parameters depend on each other. This advanced feature enables sophisticated type level programming and is used in some numerical computing applications.

Understanding parametric methods is crucial when working with Julia's type system. Methods can be specialized for specific type parameters, allowing for highly optimized code paths while maintaining generic interfaces. This is one of the key mechanisms behind Julia's performance.

Type inference in Julia is sophisticated and usually automatic, but you can help the compiler by providing type annotations in function signatures or variable declarations. While not always necessary, strategic type annotations can improve performance and code clarity.

The type system includes support for abstract arrays and other abstract collections, allowing you to create new collection types that automatically work with existing code. This extensibility is one of Julia's great strengths for numerical computing and data science applications.

Error handling in the type system is generally clear and helpful. Type assertions and bounds checking help catch errors early, while informative error messages help diagnose type related issues. The @code_warntype macro is particularly useful for identifying type stability issues.

Understanding Julia's type system is essential for writing efficient code and taking full advantage of multiple dispatch, which we'll explore in the next chapter. The type system provides the foundation for Julia's performance and expressiveness, making it a crucial topic for any data scientist working with Julia.

Chapter 6: Multiple Dispatch and Its Power

Multiple dispatch is a fundamental feature of Julia that sets it apart from traditional object oriented programming languages. Unlike in Python or R where method calls are resolved based on a single argument (the object on which the method is called), Julia can dispatch to different method implementations based on the types of all arguments. This powerful feature enables elegant and efficient solutions to many computational problems.

Let's start with a basic example to understand multiple dispatch. Consider a function add that works with different numeric types. In Julia, you can define multiple methods for the same function name, each handling different type combinations: add(x::Int64, y::Int64) = x + y; add(x::Float64, y::Float64) = x + y; add(x::String, y::String) = string(x, y). When you call add(1, 2), Julia automatically selects the first method because both arguments are integers. This selection happens at compile time, making it very efficient.

The real power of multiple dispatch becomes apparent when working with complex type hierarchies. Consider scientific computing where you might have different types of matrices: dense matrices, sparse matrices, and structured matrices like diagonal or triangular matrices. With multiple dispatch, you can write specialized implementations of operations like multiplication that take advantage of the specific properties of each matrix type. The correct implementation is automatically selected based on the types of the matrices involved.

Multiple dispatch also enables a form of programming called expression problem solution. This refers to the ability to add both new types and new operations without modifying existing code. In traditional object oriented programming, adding new operations requires modifying all existing classes. With multiple dispatch, you can simply define new methods for existing functions that handle your new types.

One of the key benefits of multiple dispatch is code organization. Instead of spreading related functionality across different classes, you can group related methods together. This makes the code more maintainable and easier to understand. For example, all methods related to matrix multiplication can be kept together, regardless of the specific matrix types they handle.

Type promotion is another area where multiple dispatch shines. When performing operations on mixed types (like adding an integer and a float), Julia uses multiple dispatch to automatically select the appropriate method after promoting the arguments to a common type. This system is extensible you can define your own promotion rules for custom types.

The combination of multiple dispatch and Julia's type system enables powerful generic programming patterns. You can write algorithms that work with any type satisfying certain abstract interfaces, and Julia will automatically select the most specific implementation available. This leads to code that is both generic and efficient.

Performance is a key advantage of multiple dispatch. Because method selection happens at compile time, there's no runtime overhead for dispatch. The compiler can generate specialized code for each combination of argument types, leading to excellent performance. This is particularly important in numerical computing and data science applications where performance is critical.

Method ambiguity is an important consideration when working with multiple dispatch. If there are multiple methods that could handle a given set of arguments, Julia will throw a MethodError. This is actually helpful as it forces you to be explicit about which method should handle which cases. You can resolve ambiguities by defining more specific methods or by using type constraints.

Multiple dispatch enables a programming style that focuses on behaviors rather than objects. Instead of thinking about what methods belong to which objects, you think about what operations make sense for different combinations of types. This leads to more natural abstractions for many problems, particularly in scientific computing.

The concept of holy traits, named by Tim Holy, is a powerful pattern enabled by multiple dispatch. It allows you to dispatch on properties of types rather than the types themselves. For example, you might want different behavior for types that are iteratable versus those that aren't. You can accomplish this by defining trait types and methods that dispatch on them.

Multiple dispatch works seamlessly with Julia's parametric types. You can define methods that work with any type parameter, as well as methods specialized for specific type parameters. This combination enables both generic code and optimized implementations for specific cases.

When working with multiple dispatch, it's important to understand method specificity. When multiple methods could apply to a given call, Julia chooses the most specific one. The specificity rules are well defined: concrete types are more specific than abstract types, and subtypes are more specific than their supertypes.

Multiple dispatch enables powerful metaprogramming patterns. You can generate methods programmatically, specialize methods for specific type combinations, and even define methods that dispatch on the types of type parameters. This flexibility is particularly useful when writing generic numerical algorithms.

Error handling in multiple dispatch is straightforward. If no method matches the types of the arguments in a function call, Julia throws a MethodError with a helpful message indicating what types were given and what methods are available. This makes debugging dispatch related issues relatively straightforward.

Multiple dispatch plays a crucial role in Julia's package ecosystem. Packages can extend existing functions with new methods for their types, enabling seamless interoperability. For example, different matrix types from different packages can all work together because they all implement the necessary methods for common operations.

Understanding multiple dispatch is essential for writing efficient Julia code. It enables you to write generic code that can handle many different types while still achieving excellent performance through specialized implementations. This combination of genericity and performance is particularly valuable in data science applications where you need to handle different types of data and computations efficiently.

The real world impact of multiple dispatch becomes clear when working with large data science projects. It allows you to write algorithms that naturally adapt to different data types and structures, while maintaining both code clarity and performance. Whether you're working with different types of arrays, implementing custom statistical methods, or building machine learning algorithms, multiple dispatch provides a powerful tool for organizing and optimizing your code.

Chapter 7: DataFrames.jl Essentials

DataFrames.jl is the cornerstone package for data manipulation in Julia, providing functionality similar to pandas in Python or dplyr in R. The package implements a powerful and efficient interface for working with tabular data, combining Julia's performance capabilities with an intuitive API for data scientists.

At its core, a DataFrame in Julia is a two-dimensional table where each column can contain data of different types. Creating a DataFrame is straightforward. You can construct one from arrays, dictionaries, or other data structures. For example, DataFrame(A = 1:4, B = ["M", "F", "F", "M"]) creates a simple DataFrame with two columns: A containing integers and B containing strings. This flexibility in column types is one of the key strengths of DataFrames.jl, leveraging Julia's type system to provide both type safety and performance.

The package provides comprehensive functionality for data manipulation. Basic operations include selecting columns (df.column_name or df[:, :column_name]), filtering rows (filter(row -> row.A > 2, df)), and adding new columns (df.new_column = calculation). These operations are designed to be both intuitive for newcomers and powerful enough for complex data manipulation tasks.

Grouping and aggregation operations are essential for data analysis. The groupby function creates a GroupedDataFrame object that can be used with various aggregation functions. For example, combine(groupby(df, :category), :value => mean) computes the mean of the value column for each category. The package supports multiple aggregation functions and allows you to define custom ones, providing great flexibility for different analysis needs.

Joining operations in DataFrames.jl are both powerful and performant. The package supports various types of joins (inner, outer, left, right) through functions like innerjoin, outerjoin, leftjoin, and rightjoin. These operations are optimized for performance and can handle large datasets efficiently. The syntax is straightforward: innerjoin(df1, df2, on = :key) joins two DataFrames on a common key column.

Data transformation is another strength of DataFrames.jl. The transform function allows you to create new columns based on existing ones, while select enables you to choose and modify columns in one operation. These functions support both simple operations and complex transformations involving multiple columns. The package also provides broadcasting capabilities, allowing you to apply functions element-wise across columns efficiently.

Missing values, a common challenge in data analysis, are handled elegantly in DataFrames.jl through Julia's built-in Missing type. The package provides functions like dropmissing and allowmissing to manage missing values, along with functions like coalesce to replace them. Operations automatically propagate missing values appropriately, making it safe to work with incomplete data.

Column operations in DataFrames.jl are type-stable and efficient. When you perform operations on columns, the package maintains type information, allowing Julia's compiler to generate optimized code. This results in better performance compared to systems where type information is lost during operations. The package also provides optimized implementations for common operations on columns.

Working with categorical data is straightforward using the CategoricalArray type, which is well integrated with DataFrames.jl. This type provides memory-efficient storage for repeated values and maintains level information for factors. Operations like frequency counting and level reordering are efficiently implemented for categorical columns.

The package includes powerful reshaping capabilities through the stack and unstack functions. These allow you to convert between wide and long formats, essential for many data analysis tasks. The implementation is both flexible and performant, handling complex reshaping operations efficiently even with large datasets.

Statistical operations are well supported in DataFrames.jl. The describe function provides summary statistics for numerical columns, while other functions enable various statistical computations on grouped data. The package integrates well with Julia's statistics ecosystem, making it easy to perform advanced statistical analyses on your data.

Performance optimization in DataFrames.jl leverages Julia's multiple dispatch system. Operations are specialized for different column types, ensuring efficient execution. The package also implements various optimization techniques like view-based operations and lazy evaluation where appropriate, reducing memory usage and improving performance.

Working with large datasets is efficient thanks to careful memory management and optimized algorithms. The package implements various strategies to minimize memory allocation and maximize performance. Operations like filtering and grouping are implemented using efficient algorithms that scale well with dataset size.

Integration with other Julia packages is seamless. DataFrames.jl works well with plotting packages, machine learning frameworks, and statistical computing packages. This ecosystem integration makes it a powerful foundation for data science workflows in Julia.

The package provides extensive support for importing and exporting data. While detailed file I/O operations are typically handled by companion packages like CSV.jl, DataFrames.jl provides the core data structures and manipulation capabilities that make working with external data efficient.

Advanced features include support for multi-index operations, complex grouping operations, and window functions. These capabilities enable sophisticated data analysis workflows comparable to what's available in other data science ecosystems, while maintaining Julia's performance advantages.

Error handling in DataFrames.jl is robust and informative. The package provides clear error messages when operations fail, making it easier to debug issues in your data manipulation code. It also includes various assertion checks to catch common mistakes early in the development process.

The package documentation is comprehensive and includes numerous examples. This makes it easier for users transitioning from other data science ecosystems to learn and adopt DataFrames.jl effectively. The documentation also includes performance tips and best practices for working with large datasets.

Understanding DataFrames.jl is crucial for productive data science work in Julia. The package provides the fundamental tools needed for data manipulation and analysis, combining ease of use with Julia's performance capabilities. Whether you're working on small analytical tasks or large-scale data processing, DataFrames.jl offers the functionality and performance needed for professional data science work.

Chapter 8: File I/O and Data Import/ Export

Working with files and managing data input/output operations efficiently is crucial for any data science workflow. Julia provides robust capabilities for handling various file formats and data exchange scenarios, combining ease of use with high performance.

The basic file operations in Julia are handled through the built-in Base module. For reading and writing text files, Julia provides simple functions like read, write, and open. The open function is particularly versatile, supporting different modes for file access. When working with text files, it's common to use the do block syntax, which ensures proper file handling and cleanup: open("filename.txt", "r") do file content = read(file, String) end. This pattern automatically closes the file when operations are complete.

CSV files are perhaps the most common format in data science, and Julia's CSV.jl package provides excellent support for working with them. The package offers high performance parsing and writing capabilities. Reading a CSV file is as simple as using CSV.read("data.csv", DataFrame), which returns a DataFrame. The CSV.jl package provides numerous options for controlling how data is parsed, including delimiter specification, header handling, and type inference. For writing DataFrames to CSV files, CSV.write("output.csv", df) provides similar flexibility in controlling the output format.

When working with Excel files, the XLSX.jl package offers comprehensive functionality. Reading an Excel file can be done with XLSX.readdata("file.xlsx", "Sheet1!A1:C10") for specific ranges, or XLSX.readtable("file.xlsx", "Sheet1") for entire sheets. The package supports reading multiple sheets, handling formulas, and preserving cell formatting. Writing to Excel files is equally well supported, with options to control cell formatting and worksheet organization.

For JSON data, a common format in web applications and APIs, the JSON.jl package provides fast and flexible parsing capabilities. The package can handle both reading from and writing to JSON format, with support for custom serialization rules. Reading JSON is straightforward: json_data = JSON.parse(read("data.json", String)). The package also supports streaming operations for handling large JSON files efficiently.

Binary data formats are essential for scientific computing applications. Julia provides native support for reading and writing binary data through functions like read and write, with control over byte ordering and data types. For more specialized binary formats, packages like HDF5.jl provide interfaces to hierarchical data formats commonly used in scientific computing. HDF5 files can store large datasets efficiently and support partial reading and writing operations.

Database connectivity is another crucial aspect of data I/O. Julia offers several packages for database integration. For SQL databases, packages like SQLite.jl, MySQL.jl, and PostgreSQL.jl provide native Julia interfaces to their respective databases. These packages support both basic query operations and bulk data transfer, often with support for converting between database tables and DataFrames.

When working with remote data sources, Julia's HTTP.jl package provides functionality for making HTTP requests and handling responses. This is particularly useful for working with web APIs and downloading data files. The package supports various HTTP methods, header manipulation, and handling of different response types.

For handling compressed files, Julia provides integration with common compression formats through packages like GZip.jl and ZIP.jl. These packages allow reading and writing compressed files transparently, often with support for streaming operations to handle large files efficiently.

Data serialization is important for storing Julia objects and sharing them between different Julia processes. The built-in Serialization module provides basic functionality, while packages like JLD2.jl offer more advanced features for storing Julia objects in a format that preserves type information and handles complex object structures.

When working with image files, packages like Images.jl provide comprehensive support for various image formats. The package can read and write common image formats like PNG, JPEG, and TIFF, while preserving metadata and handling color space conversions.

For time series data, specialized packages like TimeseriesIO.jl provide support for formats commonly used in financial and scientific applications. These packages often include functionality for handling different time zone specifications and data alignment issues.

Memory mapping can be crucial when working with large files that don't fit in memory. Julia's Mmap module provides support for memory-mapped I/O, allowing you to work with large files as if they were in memory, while actually reading and writing data to disk as needed.

Error handling in file I/O operations requires careful consideration. Julia's exception handling system allows you to catch and handle various types of I/O errors gracefully. It's important to use try-catch blocks when working with files to ensure proper error recovery and resource cleanup.

Performance optimization for file I/O often involves careful buffer management and choosing appropriate chunk sizes for reading and writing operations. Julia provides various tools for controlling these aspects, including support for buffered I/O and asynchronous operations.

Working with streaming data requires different approaches than handling files. Julia provides support for various streaming protocols and data formats through packages like Sockets.jl for network streams and CSV.jl's streaming capabilities for handling large text files.

When dealing with sensitive data, it's important to consider security aspects of file I/O. Julia provides functionality for handling file permissions and encryption through various packages. Always ensure proper handling of credentials and sensitive information when working with protected data sources.

Integration with cloud storage services is increasingly important for data science workflows. Packages like AWSS3.jl and GoogleCloud.jl provide interfaces to popular cloud storage services, allowing you to read and write data directly to cloud storage.

Version control for data files can be managed through packages like DataDeps.jl, which helps manage and version data dependencies in your projects. This is particularly useful for ensuring reproducibility in data science workflows.

Understanding these various aspects of file I/O and data import/export capabilities is essential for building robust data science applications in Julia. The ecosystem provides comprehensive tools for handling different data formats and storage systems, while maintaining Julia's focus on performance and ease of use.

Chapter 9: Data Cleaning and Preprocessing

Data cleaning and preprocessing are fundamental steps in any data science workflow, often consuming a significant portion of a data scientist's time. Julia provides powerful tools and packages for handling these tasks efficiently while maintaining high performance.

The first step in data cleaning often involves handling missing values. Julia represents missing values using the Missing type, which propagates through calculations in a way that prevents silent errors. The Missings.jl package provides additional functionality for working with missing values. You can detect missing values using ismissing() and handle them using functions like dropmissing() to remove rows with missing values, or replace them using replace() with specific values or functions.

For example, when working with a DataFrame, you might encounter various patterns of missing data. Some columns might have systematic missing values, while others might have random occurrences. Julia's DataFrames.jl provides several approaches to handle these situations. The completecases() function helps identify rows with complete data across specified columns, while coalesce() can be used to replace missing values with defaults in a type-stable way.

Outlier detection and handling is another crucial aspect of data cleaning. Julia's Statistics module provides functions for calculating basic statistical measures that can help identify outliers. The Distributions.jl package offers additional tools for more sophisticated outlier detection methods, such as fitting probability distributions and calculating z-scores. You can implement methods like the Interquartile Range (IQR) rule or use more advanced techniques like Isolation Forests through packages like OutlierDetection.jl.

Data type conversion and validation are essential preprocessing steps. Julia's strong type system helps catch many errors early, but you often need to clean and convert data types explicitly. The DataFrames.jl package provides functions like transform() and select() for applying type conversions across columns. The CSV.jl package offers options for specifying column types during data import, helping ensure data consistency from the start.

String cleaning and standardization are common requirements, especially when working with text data. Julia's built-in string functions provide powerful tools for text manipulation. Regular expressions in Julia are both expressive and fast, making them excellent for pattern matching and replacement. The TextAnalysis.jl package offers additional functionality for text preprocessing, including case normalization, whitespace handling, and special character removal.

Feature scaling and normalization are crucial for many machine learning algorithms. Julia's MLJ.jl ecosystem provides transformers for various scaling methods, including standardization (z-score normalization) and min-max scaling. These transformers can be applied individually or integrated into machine learning pipelines, ensuring consistent preprocessing across training and test data.

Categorical variable encoding is another important preprocessing step. Julia's CategoricalArrays.jl package provides robust support for working with categorical data, including both nominal and ordinal variables. The package handles level encoding, compression of string categories, and missing value support. For machine learning applications, you can easily convert categorical variables to dummy variables using MLJ.jl's encoders.

Time series data often requires specific preprocessing steps. Julia's Dates module provides comprehensive functionality for working with temporal data. The TimeArrays.jl package offers additional tools for time series manipulation, including alignment, resampling, and handling of missing timestamps. For financial time series, BusinessDays.jl helps handle business day calculations and adjustments.

Data aggregation and reshaping are common preprocessing tasks. DataFrames.jl provides powerful functions like groupby() for aggregation and combine() for applying functions to grouped data. The package also supports various forms of joining and merging operations, making it easy to combine data from different sources while handling key matching and type compatibility.

Feature engineering often requires custom transformations. Julia's broadcast syntax (dot operators) makes it easy to apply functions element-wise across arrays and DataFrames. The Chain.jl package provides a convenient pipeline syntax for combining multiple transformation steps. For more complex feature engineering, you can define custom types and methods that integrate seamlessly with Julia's type system.

Data validation and quality checks are essential for maintaining data integrity. The DataFramesMeta.jl package provides a convenient macro-based syntax for expressing complex data validation rules. You can create custom validation functions that check for business rules, data constraints, and logical consistency across columns.

When working with large datasets, memory efficiency becomes important. Julia's views and memory-efficient operations help manage memory usage during preprocessing. The OnlineStats.jl package provides algorithms for processing data in a streaming fashion, allowing you to handle datasets that don't fit in memory.

Error handling during preprocessing requires careful consideration. Julia's exception system allows you to catch and handle specific error types, making it possible to build robust preprocessing pipelines that can handle unexpected data issues gracefully. Logging preprocessing steps and errors helps with debugging and audit trails.

Performance optimization in preprocessing often involves vectorization and careful memory management. Julia's multiple dispatch system allows you to write generic preprocessing functions that automatically optimize for different data types. The ThreadsX.jl package can help parallelize preprocessing operations when working with large datasets.

Data imputation for missing values can be handled through various approaches. The Impute.jl package provides several imputation methods, from simple mean/median imputation to more sophisticated methods like k-nearest neighbors imputation. For time series data, specialized imputation methods can account for temporal dependencies.

Handling duplicates is another common preprocessing task. DataFrames.jl provides functions like unique() and duplicated() for identifying and removing duplicate rows. You can specify multiple columns for determining uniqueness and control how duplicates are handled.

Data anonymization and privacy preservation might be required for sensitive datasets. Julia packages provide tools for various anonymization techniques, including hashing, encryption, and data masking. When working with personal data, it's important to implement appropriate privacy-preserving preprocessing steps.

Documentation of preprocessing steps is crucial for reproducibility. Julia's documentation system allows you to create detailed documentation for custom preprocessing functions and pipelines. Using notebooks or literate programming tools like Literate.jl can help create self-documenting preprocessing workflows.

Version control for preprocessing pipelines helps track changes and ensure consistency. Using git for code version control, combined with data versioning tools, helps maintain a complete history of how data has been processed and transformed.

Integration with other tools in the data science ecosystem is often necessary. Julia's interoperability with Python and R allows you to leverage existing preprocessing tools from those ecosystems when needed, while maintaining the performance benefits of native Julia implementations.

Chapter 10: Data Visualization with Plots.jl

Here's Chapter 10 on Data Visualization with Plots.jl:

Data visualization is a crucial component of data science, enabling both exploratory data analysis and effective communication of results. Julia's Plots.jl ecosystem provides a powerful and flexible framework for creating publication quality visualizations while maintaining the language's performance advantages.

Plots.jl serves as a unified interface to multiple plotting backends, allowing users to switch between different visualization engines without changing their code. The most commonly used backends include GR for speed, PyPlot for matplotlib compatibility, and PlotlyJS for interactive web based visualizations. You can select a backend using the command using Plots; gr() or similar commands for other backends.

Creating basic plots in Julia is straightforward. The plot() function serves as the primary entry point for most visualizations. For example, to create a line plot, you can simply pass arrays of x and y coordinates: plot(x, y). The resulting plot can be customized with various attributes like line style, color, width, and markers. These attributes can be specified using keyword arguments or through the plot attribute macro @.

Plots.jl supports multiple series in a single plot through several approaches. You can use the plot!() function to add series to an existing plot, or pass multiple series to the initial plot() call. The package automatically assigns different colors and styles to each series for clear differentiation. Labels for multiple series can be specified using the label keyword argument, and a legend is automatically generated.

Statistical visualizations are essential for data science work. Plots.jl provides functions for creating histograms (histogram()), box plots (boxplot()), violin plots (violin()), and scatter plots (scatter()). These functions integrate well with statistical computations, making it easy

to visualize distributions and relationships in your data. For density estimation, the density() function creates smooth kernel density plots.

For more complex visualizations, Plots.jl supports subplots and layouts. The layout keyword argument allows you to arrange multiple plots in a grid, while subplot() provides fine grained control over plot placement. The @layout macro enables creation of complex custom layouts with different sized plots arranged in various patterns.

Color schemes play a crucial role in effective visualization. Plots.jl provides access to numerous predefined color palettes and supports custom color specifications. Colors can be specified using names, RGB values, or hex codes. The package also supports color gradients for continuous color scales, useful for heatmaps and surface plots.

Three dimensional visualization capabilities in Plots.jl include surface plots (surface()), wireframe plots (wireframe()), and scatter plots in 3D space (scatter3d()). These visualizations can be rotated and viewed from different angles interactively when using appropriate backends. The package handles perspective and lighting automatically, though these can be customized if needed.

Animation support in Plots.jl enables creation of dynamic visualizations. The @animate macro simplifies the process of creating animations frame by frame. Animations can be saved in various formats including GIF and MP4. This functionality is particularly useful for visualizing time series data or algorithm behavior over time.

When working with statistical plots, error bars and confidence intervals are often necessary. Plots.jl provides several ways to represent uncertainty, including traditional error bars (yerror, xerror keywords), ribbon plots (ribbon keyword), and custom error representations. These can be combined with other plot types to create comprehensive statistical visualizations.

Geographic visualization is supported through various packages that integrate with Plots.jl. The GeoMakie.jl package, while technically part of a different ecosystem, provides excellent geographic plotting capabilities. For simpler geographic visualizations, Plots.jl can handle coordinate systems and projections directly.

Interactive features become available when using backends like PlotlyJS. These include zoom, pan, hover tooltips, and click events. Such interactivity is particularly valuable during exploratory data analysis, allowing users to examine details of their data dynamically.

Font handling and text rendering in Plots.jl support multiple fonts, sizes, and styles. LaTeX expressions can be included in plot text using LaTeXStrings.jl, enabling proper rendering of mathematical notation in titles, labels, and annotations. This is particularly useful for scientific visualization.

Performance considerations become important when creating visualizations for large datasets. Plots.jl implements various optimization strategies, including downsampling for large datasets and efficient rendering algorithms. The GR backend is particularly well suited for handling large datasets efficiently.

Saving plots in various formats is straightforward with Plots.jl. The savefig() function supports multiple output formats including PNG, PDF, SVG, and EPS. Vector formats like PDF and SVG are particularly useful for publication quality graphics that can be scaled without loss of quality.

Theme customization allows you to maintain consistent styling across multiple plots. Plots.jl provides theme support through the theme() function, allowing you to set default values for various plot attributes. Custom themes can be created and shared across projects for consistent visualization styles.

Integration with DataFrames.jl is seamless, with direct plotting support for DataFrame columns. The @df macro provides a convenient syntax for creating plots directly from DataFrames, automatically handling column names and data access.

Recipe system in Plots.jl enables extension of plotting capabilities for custom types. By defining recipe functions, you can specify how

your custom types should be visualized, making them work naturally with the plotting interface. This extensibility is particularly valuable when working with domain specific data types.

Composite plots combining different plot types can be created using the plot() function with multiple series of different types. This allows creation of complex visualizations that combine, for example, scatter plots with line plots or bar charts with error bars.

Best practices for data visualization include choosing appropriate plot types for different data and analysis goals, maintaining consistent styling, and ensuring accessibility through proper color choices and clear labeling. Plots.jl provides the tools necessary to implement these best practices effectively.

The ecosystem around Plots.jl continues to grow, with specialized packages building on its foundation to provide additional visualization capabilities. These include StatsPlots.jl for statistical visualizations, GraphPlots.jl for network visualization, and various domain specific visualization packages.

Chapter 11: Statistical Computing Basics

Statistical computing forms the backbone of data science, and Julia provides robust tools for performing statistical analyses efficiently. The Statistics standard library, along with packages like StatsBase.jl, HypothesisTests.jl, and Distributions.jl, offers comprehensive functionality for statistical computing.

Basic descriptive statistics in Julia can be computed using functions from the Statistics standard library. These include mean(), median(), std() for standard deviation, var() for variance, and quantile() for calculating percentiles. These functions are optimized for performance and work seamlessly with various data structures including arrays and DataFrames columns.

The StatsBase.jl package extends these capabilities with additional statistical functions. It provides tools for computing weighted statistics, correlation coefficients, covariance matrices, and various measures of central tendency and dispersion. The package also includes functions for sampling, ranking, and computing order statistics.

Probability distributions are handled through the Distributions.jl package, which provides a comprehensive framework for working with probability distributions. The package supports a wide range of continuous and discrete distributions, including normal, uniform, binomial, Poisson, and many others. Each distribution type is implemented as a concrete type, allowing for efficient computation and type stability.

Creating distribution objects is straightforward. For example, a normal distribution can be created with Normal(μ, σ), where μ is the mean and σ is the standard deviation. The package provides methods for computing probability density functions (pdf), cumulative distribution functions (cdf), quantiles (quantile), and random sampling (rand) for all supported distributions.

Hypothesis testing is implemented in the HypothesisTests.jl package, which provides a wide range of statistical tests. Common tests include t tests, chi square tests, Kolmogorov Smirnov tests, and many others. The package uses a consistent interface across different tests, making it easy to perform and interpret statistical analyses.

When performing hypothesis tests, results are returned as test objects that contain all relevant information about the test, including test statistics, p values, and confidence intervals. These objects can be displayed in a human readable format or accessed programmatically for further analysis or reporting.

Random number generation in Julia is both flexible and efficient. The Random standard library provides various random number generators and methods for generating random values from different distributions. The SIMD optimized generators ensure high performance when generating large quantities of random numbers.

Bootstrap methods and resampling techniques can be implemented efficiently in Julia due to its performance characteristics. The Bootstrap.jl package provides tools for bootstrap sampling and analysis, including various bootstrap confidence interval methods and bootstrap hypothesis tests.

Regression analysis is supported through multiple packages. The GLM.jl package provides tools for fitting and analyzing generalized linear models, including linear regression, logistic regression, and Poisson regression. The package integrates well with the DataFrame ecosystem and provides methods for model diagnostics and inference.

Model fitting in GLM.jl follows a familiar formula interface similar to R, making it accessible to users coming from R. The resulting model objects contain comprehensive information about the fit, including coefficient estimates, standard errors, and various goodness of fit statistics.

Robust statistics are implemented in packages like RobustStats.jl, which provides methods for statistical analysis that are less sensitive to outliers and violations of distributional assumptions. This includes robust estimation methods and robust hypothesis tests.

Time series analysis basics are supported through various statistical functions that can be applied to time series data. This includes autocorrelation functions, partial autocorrelation functions, and basic time series decomposition methods.

Categorical data analysis is facilitated through specialized functions in StatsBase.jl and related packages. This includes methods for computing contingency tables, chi square tests, and various measures of association for categorical variables.

Nonparametric statistics are well supported, with implementations of various rank based tests and methods that do not assume specific probability distributions. This includes the Wilcoxon rank sum test, Kruskal Wallis test, and kernel density estimation.

Multivariate statistics are handled through packages like MultivariateStats.jl, which provides implementations of principal component analysis, factor analysis, canonical correlation analysis, and other multivariate techniques.

Statistical power analysis can be performed using various functions for computing sample size requirements and power calculations. This is particularly important for experimental design and ensuring adequate statistical power in studies.

Bayesian statistics basics are supported through packages like Turing.jl, though more advanced Bayesian methods are typically handled by specialized packages. Basic conjugate prior analyses and simple Bayesian computations can be performed using core statistical functions.

Performance considerations are important in statistical computing, and Julia's implementation ensures efficient computation even with large datasets. Many statistical functions are optimized for parallel execution when appropriate.

Integration with other statistical packages is possible through various interface packages. This allows users to leverage existing R and Python statistical libraries while maintaining Julia's performance advantages where possible.

Error handling in statistical computations is robust, with appropriate warnings and errors raised when statistical assumptions are violated or computational problems arise. This helps ensure reliable statistical analyses.

The statistical computing ecosystem in Julia continues to grow, with new packages and methods being added regularly. The strong type system and multiple dispatch capabilities of Julia make it particularly well suited for implementing new statistical methods and algorithms.

Visualization of statistical results is seamlessly integrated with the plotting capabilities discussed in the previous chapter, allowing for creation of statistical graphics and diagnostic plots. This integration facilitates comprehensive statistical analysis workflows.

Documentation and examples for statistical computing in Julia are extensive, with detailed documentation available for all major packages and functions. This includes theoretical background, usage examples, and best practices for statistical analysis.

Chapter 12: Linear Algebra Operations

Linear algebra operations are fundamental to many data science and scientific computing applications, and Julia excels in this domain with its native support for linear algebra operations and powerful packages like LinearAlgebra, which is part of Julia's standard library. The language's design makes it particularly well suited for expressing linear algebra computations in a way that is both intuitive and computationally efficient.

Matrix operations in Julia are straightforward and efficient. Creating matrices can be done using several methods, from direct construction using array literals to specialized functions like zeros(), ones(), and rand(). The language supports various matrix types, including dense matrices, sparse matrices, and special matrix structures like symmetric, triangular, or diagonal matrices.

Basic arithmetic operations on matrices follow natural mathematical notation. Matrix addition, subtraction, and scalar multiplication work exactly as you would expect, using standard operators. Matrix multiplication is performed using the * operator, while element wise multiplication uses the .* operator. This distinction between matrix and element wise operations is consistent across all operations in Julia.

The LinearAlgebra package provides a comprehensive set of functions for matrix decompositions, which are crucial for many numerical algorithms. These include LU decomposition (lu), QR decomposition (qr), Cholesky decomposition (cholesky), and singular value decomposition (svd). Each decomposition is implemented efficiently and returns a factorization object that can be used for further computations.

Eigenvalue and eigenvector computations are handled through the eigen function, which returns both eigenvalues and eigenvectors. For symmetric matrices, there's a specialized eigvals function that computes only the eigenvalues, which can be more efficient when eigenvectors aren't needed. The package also provides methods for computing generalized eigenvalue problems.

Matrix inversion and solving linear systems are fundamental operations that Julia handles efficiently. The inv function computes matrix inverses, while the \ operator (backslash) provides a more numerically stable way to solve linear systems. The backslash operator automatically chooses the most appropriate algorithm based on the matrix structure, making it both efficient and numerically stable.

Special matrix types in Julia deserve special attention. The language provides optimized implementations for symmetric matrices (Symmetric), Hermitian matrices (Hermitian), triangular matrices (UpperTriangular and LowerTriangular), and diagonal matrices (Diagonal). Using these specialized types when appropriate can lead to significant performance improvements and better numerical stability.

Sparse matrix operations are supported through the SparseArrays standard library. Sparse matrices are essential for working with large, sparse datasets efficiently. Julia provides specialized algorithms for sparse matrix operations and decompositions, making it possible to work with very large sparse systems efficiently.

Vector operations are equally well supported. Julia provides efficient implementations of vector arithmetic, dot products (dot or ·), cross products (cross), and various vector norms. The language also supports broadcasting operations, making it easy to apply functions element wise to vectors and matrices.

Matrix factorizations play a crucial role in many numerical algorithms. Julia's implementation of matrix factorizations is both efficient and user friendly. The factorization objects returned by decomposition functions can be reused for multiple computations, saving computational resources when solving multiple related problems.

Numerical stability is a key consideration in linear algebra computations. Julia's linear algebra implementations include various techniques to ensure numerical stability, such as pivoting in LU decomposition and iterative refinement in linear system solving. The language also provides condition number calculations to help assess the numerical stability of matrix operations.

Performance optimization in linear algebra operations is achieved through multiple mechanisms. Julia uses BLAS and LAPACK under the hood for many operations, ensuring high performance for standard linear algebra computations. The language also provides ways to use specialized hardware like GPUs for linear algebra operations through packages like CUDA.jl.

Working with large matrices requires careful memory management. Julia provides various tools for handling large linear algebra problems efficiently, including views into matrices (view), which allow operating on portions of matrices without creating copies, and in place operations for modifying matrices without allocating new memory.

The integration of linear algebra operations with Julia's type system is particularly elegant. The multiple dispatch system allows for specialized implementations of algorithms based on matrix structure and element type, leading to both clean code and optimal performance. This integration extends to user defined types, making it possible to create custom matrix types that work seamlessly with existing linear algebra functions.

Advanced linear algebra operations such as generalized eigenvalue problems, matrix functions (like matrix exponential or matrix logarithm), and matrix equations (like Sylvester and Lyapunov equations) are also supported through various packages in the Julia ecosystem.

Error handling in linear algebra operations is robust, with appropriate exceptions raised for singular matrices, dimension mismatches, and other common problems. The error messages are informative and help users identify and fix issues in their linear algebra computations.

The performance of linear algebra operations in Julia is competitive with or superior to other numerical computing environments. This is particularly important for data science applications, where linear algebra operations often form the computational bottleneck.

The integration with other parts of the Julia ecosystem is seamless. Linear algebra operations work naturally with the array programming features of the language and integrate well with other numerical computing packages, making it easy to build complex numerical algorithms.

Documentation for linear algebra operations in Julia is comprehensive, with detailed explanations of functions and their algorithmic properties. This includes information about computational complexity, memory usage, and numerical stability considerations.

Best practices for linear algebra in Julia include using appropriate matrix types for different problems, leveraging specialized decompositions when applicable, and being mindful of memory usage and numerical stability. Following these practices leads to efficient and reliable numerical computations.

Chapter 13: Optimization Algorithms

Optimization algorithms are central to many data science applications, from machine learning to operations research. Julia provides excellent support for optimization through various packages, with JuMP (Julia for Mathematical Programming) being one of the most prominent. This chapter explores the optimization capabilities in Julia, covering both linear and nonlinear optimization problems.

The Optim.jl package serves as a fundamental tool for unconstrained and box constrained optimization in Julia. It provides implementations of various classical optimization algorithms including gradient descent, Newton's method, BFGS, and Nelder Mead. These methods can be applied to a wide range of optimization problems, from simple function minimization to complex statistical parameter estimation.

Gradient based optimization methods form the backbone of many optimization algorithms. Julia's automatic differentiation capabilities, provided through packages like ForwardDiff.jl and ReverseDiff.jl, make it straightforward to compute gradients and Hessians automatically. This integration allows users to focus on defining their objective functions while leaving the computation of derivatives to the automatic differentiation system.

For constrained optimization problems, JuMP provides a powerful modeling language that supports both linear and nonlinear constraints. JuMP's syntax is particularly elegant, allowing users to express optimization problems in a form that closely resembles their mathematical formulation. The package supports integration with numerous solvers, both open source and commercial, making it versatile for different types of optimization problems.

Linear programming problems can be solved efficiently using JuMP in conjunction with solvers like GLPK, Clp, or commercial solvers like Gurobi and CPLEX. The syntax for defining linear programs is intuitive, with support for both equality and inequality constraints. Variables can be continuous or integer valued, allowing for mixed integer linear programming problems.

Nonlinear optimization problems require more sophisticated approaches. Julia provides several options through packages like Ipopt and NLopt. These solvers can handle problems with nonlinear objective functions and constraints, using methods like interior point optimization and sequential quadratic programming. The automatic differentiation capabilities of Julia make it particularly effective for solving nonlinear optimization problems.

Convex optimization is another important category that Julia handles well through the Convex.jl package. This package provides a domain specific language for specifying convex optimization problems, with support for many standard problem types including linear programming, quadratic programming, and semidefinite programming. The syntax is expressive and the package automatically verifies the convexity of the problem formulation.

Stochastic optimization methods are essential for problems involving uncertainty or very large datasets. Julia provides implementations of various stochastic optimization algorithms, including stochastic gradient descent and its variants. These methods are particularly important in machine learning applications, where they are used to train models on large datasets.

Global optimization problems, which involve finding the global minimum or maximum of a function that may have multiple local optima, can be approached using packages like BlackBoxOptim.jl. This package implements various global optimization algorithms, including evolutionary algorithms and particle swarm optimization.

The performance of optimization algorithms in Julia is excellent, thanks to the language's efficient implementation of numerical computations and its ability to generate specialized code through multiple dispatch. This is particularly important for large scale optimization problems, where computational efficiency is crucial.

Error handling and solution verification are important aspects of optimization. Julia's optimization packages provide detailed information about the convergence status, objective value, and solution quality. This helps users understand whether their optimization problems have been solved successfully and what might be causing any failures.

Parameter tuning is often necessary for optimization algorithms to perform well. Julia's optimization packages provide various options for controlling algorithm behavior, including convergence tolerances, iteration limits, and algorithm specific parameters. Understanding these parameters and their effects is crucial for achieving good optimization results.

Parallel and distributed optimization is supported through Julia's parallel computing capabilities. Some optimization algorithms can naturally take advantage of multiple processors, while others can be parallelized at the problem level, such as when solving multiple optimization problems with different initial conditions.

The integration of optimization with other Julia packages is seamless. Optimization problems often arise in the context of statistical modeling, machine learning, or scientific computing, and Julia's ecosystem makes it easy to combine optimization with other numerical computing tasks.

Visualization of optimization results can be helpful for understanding algorithm behavior and solution quality. Julia's plotting packages can be used to visualize objective function landscapes, constraint boundaries, and optimization trajectories.

Memory management is important when dealing with large scale optimization problems. Julia provides various tools for managing memory efficiently, including the ability to work with sparse matrices and specialized data structures for optimization problems.

Best practices for optimization in Julia include careful problem formulation, appropriate choice of optimization algorithm, proper scaling of variables and constraints, and thorough testing of solutions. Following these practices helps ensure reliable and efficient optimization results.

The ecosystem of optimization packages in Julia continues to grow, with new algorithms and capabilities being added regularly. This makes Julia an increasingly powerful platform for solving optimization problems in data science and other applications.

Documentation for optimization packages in Julia is generally excellent, with detailed examples and explanations of algorithm properties. This helps users choose appropriate methods for their problems and understand how to use them effectively.

The future of optimization in Julia looks promising, with ongoing development of new algorithms and improvements to existing ones. The language's combination of performance, ease of use, and extensive optimization capabilities makes it an excellent choice for solving optimization problems in production data science applications.

Chapter 14: Machine Learning with MLJ.jl

Machine learning has become an essential component of modern data science, and Julia's MLJ.jl framework provides a comprehensive ecosystem for building, evaluating, and deploying machine learning models. MLJ.jl stands out for its composable design, type safety, and excellent performance characteristics that make it suitable for production environments.

The MLJ.jl framework follows a modular architecture that separates machine learning models from their implementations. This design allows users to switch between different implementations of the same algorithm seamlessly, making it easy to experiment with various approaches. The framework supports a wide range of machine learning tasks, including classification, regression, clustering, and dimensionality reduction.

Getting started with MLJ.jl involves loading the necessary packages and importing the desired models. The framework provides a unified interface to many popular machine learning algorithms, including decision trees, random forests, support vector machines, and gradient boosting methods. These algorithms are implemented in various Julia packages and are made accessible through MLJ.jl's consistent interface.

Data preparation is a crucial step in any machine learning pipeline. MLJ.jl provides tools for handling missing values, encoding categorical variables, and scaling numerical features. The framework's transformation operations are type aware and can be composed into pipelines that automatically handle the preprocessing of both training and test data.

Model selection and hyperparameter tuning are well supported in MLJ.jl through its tuning interface. The framework provides various tuning strategies, including grid search, random search, and Bayesian optimization. These tuning operations can be performed efficiently, taking advantage of Julia's parallel computing capabilities to evaluate multiple parameter combinations simultaneously.

Cross validation is essential for assessing model performance, and MLJ.jl offers several cross validation strategies. Users can perform k fold cross validation, leave one out cross validation, or custom validation schemes. The framework provides detailed performance metrics and makes it easy to compare different models using consistent evaluation criteria.

Ensemble methods are powerful techniques for improving model performance, and MLJ.jl provides extensive support for building and training ensembles. Users can create homogeneous ensembles, such as random forests, or heterogeneous ensembles that combine different types of models. The framework handles the complexity of training and combining multiple models while maintaining type safety.

Feature selection is another important aspect of machine learning that MLJ.jl addresses. The framework provides various feature selection methods, from simple filters based on correlation to more sophisticated wrapper and embedded methods. These can be integrated into machine learning pipelines to automatically select the most relevant features for a given task.

Model persistence is crucial for production environments, and MLJ.jl makes it straightforward to save and load trained models. The framework ensures that all necessary information, including preprocessing steps and model parameters, is properly serialized. This makes it easy to deploy models in production systems and share them between different parts of an application.

One of MLJ.jl's strengths is its handling of probabilistic predictions. Many models in the framework can produce probability distributions rather than just point predictions, which is valuable for understanding prediction uncertainty. This probabilistic approach is particularly useful in applications where understanding prediction confidence is important.

Performance monitoring and model updating are essential in production environments. MLJ.jl provides tools for tracking model performance over time and updating models with new data. The framework's design makes it easy to implement online learning scenarios where models need to adapt to changing patterns in the data.

Integration with other Julia packages is seamless in MLJ.jl. The framework works well with DataFrames.jl for data manipulation, Plots.jl for visualization, and various optimization packages for model tuning. This integration allows users to build complete machine learning workflows within the Julia ecosystem.

MLJ.jl's type system ensures that machine learning operations are safe and well defined. The framework checks compatibility between data types and model requirements at compile time, helping to catch potential errors early in the development process. This type safety is particularly valuable in production environments where reliability is crucial.

Handling large datasets is an important consideration in production machine learning. MLJ.jl provides efficient implementations that can handle large scale data, and its integration with Julia's parallel computing capabilities allows for distributed processing when necessary. The framework also supports out of core processing for datasets that don't fit in memory.

Custom model development is well supported in MLJ.jl. The framework provides clear interfaces for implementing new machine learning algorithms, making it easy to extend its functionality. This extensibility is valuable when specialized algorithms are needed for particular applications.

Documentation and learning resources for MLJ.jl are extensive, with comprehensive guides, examples, and API documentation. The framework's design principles are well documented, making it easier for users to understand how to use it effectively and extend it when needed.

The future development of MLJ.jl continues to focus on expanding its capabilities while maintaining its commitment to type safety and performance. The framework is actively maintained and regularly updated with new features and improvements, making it a reliable choice for production machine learning applications.

Best practices for using MLJ.jl in production include proper validation of models, careful monitoring of performance metrics, and appropriate handling of model updates. The framework provides the tools needed to implement these practices effectively, helping to ensure reliable machine learning deployments.

The MLJ.jl ecosystem continues to grow with new models and capabilities being added regularly. This growth, combined with Julia's performance characteristics and the framework's robust design, makes MLJ.jl an excellent choice for production machine learning applications.

Chapter 15: Deep Learning with Flux.jl

Deep learning has revolutionized many areas of artificial intelligence, and Flux.jl stands as Julia's premier deep learning framework. Built with Julia's native features in mind, Flux.jl provides an elegant and performant approach to building neural networks that combines the simplicity of high level frameworks with the flexibility of low level control.

At its core, Flux.jl embraces Julia's multiple dispatch system to provide a natural and extensible interface for defining neural network architectures. The framework allows users to define models using familiar mathematical notation, making the code both readable and maintainable. This approach sets Flux.jl apart from other deep learning frameworks by eliminating the need for special operators or domain specific languages.

Getting started with Flux.jl involves understanding its fundamental building blocks. The framework provides a comprehensive set of layer types, including dense (fully connected) layers, convolutional layers, recurrent layers, and various activation functions. These components can be combined to create complex neural network architectures while maintaining clean and intuitive syntax.

Model definition in Flux.jl follows a straightforward pattern. Layers are defined as Julia structs and can be composed using standard function composition. This approach allows for great flexibility in model design while ensuring type stability and performance. The framework automatically handles parameter management and backpropagation, making it easy to focus on the architecture rather than implementation details.

Training neural networks in Flux.jl is streamlined through its optimizers and loss functions. The framework provides a wide range of optimization algorithms, including SGD, Adam, and RMSProp, along with common loss functions for various tasks. Custom loss functions can be easily defined using Julia's standard syntax, allowing for specialized training objectives when needed.

One of Flux.jl's strengths lies in its automatic differentiation system, which is built on top of Zygote.jl. This system provides efficient gradient computation for training neural networks while maintaining the ability to differentiate through arbitrary Julia code. This flexibility allows for complex architectures and custom training procedures that might be difficult to implement in other frameworks.

Data handling in Flux.jl is designed to be flexible and efficient. The framework works seamlessly with standard Julia arrays and provides utilities for batching and data loading. Integration with other Julia packages allows for easy preprocessing and augmentation of training data. The framework also supports custom data types through Julia's type system, making it adaptable to various data formats and structures.

GPU support is a crucial feature for deep learning, and Flux.jl provides excellent integration with CUDA.jl for GPU acceleration. Models and data can be easily moved between CPU and GPU, and the framework automatically handles the necessary conversions. This makes it straightforward to develop models on CPU and deploy them on GPU for faster training and inference.

Transfer learning is well supported in Flux.jl through its model zoo, which provides pre trained models for common tasks. These models can be easily loaded and fine tuned for specific applications, saving significant training time and computational resources. The framework's design makes it simple to freeze certain layers while training others, a common requirement in transfer learning scenarios.

Debugging deep learning models can be challenging, but Flux.jl provides several tools to help. The framework's integration with Julia's debugging tools allows for inspection of gradients and intermediate activations. Additionally, the clear error messages and stack traces help identify issues during model development and training.

Model deployment is an important consideration for production environments, and Flux.jl provides several options for saving and loading trained models. The framework supports serialization of model parameters and architecture, making it possible to deploy models in various environments. Integration with other Julia packages enables serving models through web APIs or embedding them in larger applications.

Advanced architectures like attention mechanisms and transformers can be implemented efficiently in Flux.jl. The framework's flexible design allows for complex neural network structures while maintaining good performance. This makes it suitable for state of the art deep learning research as well as practical applications.

Regularization techniques are essential for preventing overfitting, and Flux.jl provides various options including dropout, batch normalization, and weight decay. These can be easily incorporated into model architectures and training procedures. The framework also supports custom regularization approaches through its extensible design.

Performance optimization in Flux.jl benefits from Julia's compiler optimizations and type system. The framework is designed to generate efficient code that can take advantage of hardware acceleration. Users can fine tune performance through various techniques such as custom layers, specialized data structures, and optimized training loops.

Integration with visualization tools allows for monitoring training progress and model behavior. Flux.jl works well with plotting packages for visualizing loss curves, activation patterns, and model predictions. This integration helps in understanding model behavior and diagnosing training issues.

The ecosystem around Flux.jl continues to grow, with packages providing specialized functionality for various deep learning tasks. This includes tools for natural language processing, computer vision, and reinforcement learning. The framework's design makes it easy to integrate these specialized components while maintaining consistent interfaces.

Best practices for using Flux.jl in production include proper model versioning, monitoring of training metrics, and careful validation procedures. The framework provides the necessary tools to implement these practices effectively, helping ensure reliable deep learning deployments.

As deep learning continues to evolve, Flux.jl maintains its position as a powerful and flexible framework for both research and production applications. Its combination of elegant syntax, strong performance, and integration with the Julia ecosystem makes it an excellent choice for developing and deploying deep learning solutions.

Chapter 16: Time Series Analysis

Time series analysis forms a crucial component of many data science applications, from financial forecasting to sensor data processing. Julia's ecosystem provides powerful tools for handling temporal data, with packages like TimeSeriesKit.jl, TimeSeries.jl, and StatsBase.jl offering comprehensive functionality for time series manipulation and analysis.

The foundation of time series analysis in Julia starts with proper datetime handling. Julia's built in Dates module provides robust support for working with temporal data, offering various date time types and functions for manipulation. This native support is augmented by specialized packages that add domain specific functionality for time series operations.

When working with time series data, the first consideration is often data representation. Julia offers several approaches to storing temporal data, from simple arrays with datetime indices to specialized time series types. The TimeSeries.jl package, for example, provides the TimeArray type, which pairs time stamps with corresponding values while maintaining temporal ordering and providing methods for common operations.

Data preprocessing is a critical step in time series analysis. Common tasks include handling missing values, removing outliers, and dealing with irregular sampling intervals. Julia's ecosystem provides various tools for these tasks, such as interpolation functions for filling gaps, filtering methods for smoothing data, and resampling utilities for standardizing time intervals.

Seasonal decomposition is a fundamental technique in time series analysis, allowing us to separate data into trend, seasonal, and residual components. Julia packages implement various decomposition methods, including the classic additive and multiplicative models, as well as more sophisticated approaches like STL (Seasonal and Trend decomposition using Loess).

Statistical measures play a vital role in understanding time series characteristics. Julia provides efficient implementations of autocorrelation functions, partial autocorrelation functions, and various statistical tests specific to time series data. These tools help in identifying patterns, seasonality, and potential model specifications.

Time series forecasting is often implemented using traditional statistical models like ARIMA (Autoregressive Integrated Moving Average). Julia packages provide implementations of these models with interfaces that make it easy to fit models to data, perform diagnostics, and generate forecasts. The syntax is designed to be intuitive while maintaining computational efficiency.

Modern approaches to time series analysis often incorporate machine learning techniques. Julia's ecosystem seamlessly integrates traditional statistical methods with contemporary machine learning approaches. Packages like MLJ.jl provide interfaces to various time series specific algorithms, while maintaining compatibility with general purpose machine learning tools.

Feature engineering for time series data requires special consideration of temporal relationships. Julia's ecosystem includes tools for generating time based features, such as lagged values, rolling statistics, and temporal indicators. These features can be crucial for both statistical modeling and machine learning approaches.

Working with multiple time series simultaneously is common in many applications. Julia's support for multidimensional arrays and broadcasting operations makes it natural to handle multivariate time series data. Specialized packages provide additional functionality for analyzing relationships between multiple time series, including cointegration testing and vector autoregression models.

Performance considerations are particularly important when working with large time series datasets. Julia's type system and compiler optimizations ensure efficient execution of time series operations. The ecosystem provides specialized data structures and algorithms optimized for temporal data, allowing for fast processing of large scale time series.

Real time processing of time series data is supported through Julia's streaming data capabilities. The language's performance characteristics make it suitable for online analysis and forecasting, with packages providing tools for incremental model updates and streaming analytics.

Visualization is essential for understanding time series data and communicating results. Julia's plotting ecosystem, particularly Plots.jl, provides specialized functions for time series visualization, including line plots, seasonal plots, and diagnostic plots for model analysis.

Frequency domain analysis is another important aspect of time series analysis. Julia provides efficient implementations of Fourier transforms and related techniques, allowing for spectral analysis of time series data. These tools are particularly useful for identifying periodic components and filtering signals.

Working with different time zones and calendar effects requires careful handling of temporal data. Julia's datetime functionality includes robust support for time zone conversions and calendar calculations, making it straightforward to work with global time series data.

Error metrics specific to time series forecasting, such as MAPE (Mean Absolute Percentage Error) and RMSE (Root Mean Square Error), are readily available in Julia's ecosystem. These metrics help in evaluating and comparing different models and approaches.

Integration with external systems is often necessary when working with time series data in production environments. Julia provides connectors for various time series databases and data sources, allowing for efficient data ingestion and storage of temporal data.

The ecosystem continues to evolve with new packages and tools being developed to address specific time series analysis needs. This includes specialized packages for particular domains, such as financial time series analysis or environmental data processing.

Deployment of time series models in production environments requires consideration of model updating, monitoring, and scalability. Julia's ecosystem provides tools for automated model retraining, performance monitoring, and distributed processing of time series data.

As time series analysis continues to advance, Julia's combination of performance, ease of use, and comprehensive ecosystem makes it an excellent choice for both traditional statistical approaches and modern machine learning based methods for temporal data analysis.

Chapter 17: Image Processing

Image processing is a fundamental domain in data science and computer vision applications, and Julia provides robust tools and packages for handling various image processing tasks. The primary package for image processing in Julia is Images.jl, which offers comprehensive functionality for loading, manipulating, and analyzing digital images.

Working with images in Julia begins with understanding how images are represented. At their core, images are multidimensional arrays of pixel values. Julia's native array capabilities make it natural to work with image data, while Images.jl provides specialized types like Gray and RGB to handle different color spaces and image formats effectively.

Loading images in Julia is straightforward using the load function from FileIO.jl in conjunction with Images.jl. The ecosystem supports various image formats including PNG, JPEG, TIFF, and others. Once loaded, images can be displayed directly in notebooks or plotting environments, making it easy to visualize results during processing.

Basic image manipulations form the foundation of many processing pipelines. Julia provides efficient implementations of operations like resizing, rotating, and cropping. These operations take advantage of Julia's multiple dispatch system, allowing them to work seamlessly with different image types and color spaces.

Color space conversions are essential in many image processing applications. Julia's imaging ecosystem provides functions for converting between different color representations such as RGB, HSV, and LAB. These conversions maintain color accuracy while providing flexibility in how image data is processed.

Filtering operations are fundamental to image processing. Julia implements various filters including Gaussian blur, median filters, and edge detection filters. The implementation of these filters is highly optimized, taking advantage of Julia's computational efficiency while maintaining readable, high level syntax.

Morphological operations, which are crucial for shape analysis and feature detection, are well supported in Julia. Operations like dilation, erosion, opening, and closing can be applied to binary and grayscale images. These operations are particularly useful in applications like object detection and image segmentation.

Feature detection algorithms are implemented efficiently in Julia. The ecosystem provides implementations of popular algorithms like SIFT (Scale Invariant Feature Transform), SURF (Speeded Up Robust Features), and corner detection methods. These implementations leverage Julia's performance capabilities while maintaining ease of use.

Image segmentation is a critical task in many computer vision applications. Julia provides various segmentation algorithms including threshold based methods, region growing, and watershed segmentation. The ecosystem also supports modern approaches using graph based methods and machine learning techniques.

Working with image metadata is supported through Julia's imaging packages. This includes reading and writing EXIF data, handling color space information, and managing image properties. The ecosystem provides tools for preserving and manipulating this metadata throughout the processing pipeline.

Performance optimization is a key consideration in image processing applications. Julia's compiler optimizations and type system ensure efficient execution of image processing operations. The ecosystem includes specialized data structures and algorithms optimized for image data, allowing for fast processing of large images and image collections.

Integration with deep learning frameworks is seamless in Julia. Packages like Flux.jl can be used in conjunction with Images.jl to implement convolutional neural networks and other deep learning architectures for image processing tasks. This integration maintains

Julia's performance advantages while providing high level abstractions for model development.

Real time image processing is supported through Julia's performance characteristics and streaming capabilities. The language is well suited for applications requiring online processing of image streams, such as video processing or real time computer vision systems.

Visualization tools specific to image processing are available in Julia's ecosystem. These include functions for displaying image histograms, edge maps, and feature detection results. The visualization capabilities integrate well with Julia's general purpose plotting libraries.

Scientific image processing, particularly in fields like microscopy and medical imaging, is well supported in Julia. The ecosystem includes specialized packages for handling specific image formats and processing requirements common in scientific applications.

Working with large image datasets requires efficient memory management and processing strategies. Julia provides tools for batch processing, memory mapped operations, and distributed computing approaches specific to image processing tasks.

Image registration and alignment are important in many applications. Julia implements various registration algorithms, from simple rigid transformations to more complex deformable registration methods. These implementations maintain accuracy while providing good computational performance.

Quality assessment metrics for images are readily available in Julia's ecosystem. This includes measures of image quality, similarity metrics, and error measures specific to image processing applications. These metrics are essential for evaluating processing results and comparing different approaches.

Integration with external image processing libraries is possible through Julia's foreign function interface. This allows Julia programs to leverage existing C and Python libraries while maintaining the advantages of Julia's native ecosystem.

The ecosystem continues to evolve with new packages and tools being developed to address specific image processing needs. This includes specialized packages for particular domains such as medical image processing or satellite image analysis.

Deployment of image processing pipelines in production environments requires consideration of performance, scalability, and integration with other systems. Julia's ecosystem provides tools for building efficient, maintainable image processing applications that can scale to handle large volumes of image data.

Chapter 18: Text Processing and NLP

Text processing and natural language processing (NLP) represent crucial areas in data science where Julia excels through its comprehensive ecosystem of packages and tools. The primary packages for text processing in Julia include TextAnalysis.jl, Languages.jl, and WordTokenizers.jl, which together provide a robust foundation for handling textual data and implementing NLP pipelines.

Text processing in Julia begins with string manipulation capabilities built into the language's standard library. Julia provides powerful string operations including pattern matching, regular expressions, and substring operations. These foundational capabilities are enhanced by specialized text processing packages that add domain specific functionality.

The TextAnalysis.jl package serves as the cornerstone for many NLP tasks in Julia. It provides essential functionality for text preprocessing, including tokenization, stemming, and lemmatization. The package implements various document types and document term matrix representations, making it easy to work with collections of texts in a structured manner.

Tokenization is a fundamental operation in text processing, and Julia offers multiple approaches through WordTokenizers.jl. The package provides implementations of various tokenization algorithms, including rule based tokenizers and more sophisticated approaches that handle different languages and writing systems. The tokenization process can be customized to specific needs while maintaining high performance.

Language detection and handling multilingual text is supported through Languages.jl. This package provides capabilities for identifying text language, handling character encodings, and processing text in different writing systems. The implementation is efficient and supports a wide range of languages and scripts.

Text normalization is crucial in many NLP applications. Julia's ecosystem includes tools for case normalization, punctuation handling, and special character processing. These operations can be combined into custom preprocessing pipelines that maintain the efficiency characteristics of Julia while providing flexibility in handling different text processing requirements.

Part of speech tagging and syntactic parsing are implemented through various packages in the Julia ecosystem. These implementations leverage modern NLP algorithms while taking advantage of Julia's performance capabilities. The ecosystem supports both rule based and statistical approaches to linguistic analysis.

Named entity recognition (NER) capabilities are available through specialized packages. These implementations support the identification and classification of entities such as names, organizations, and locations in text. The ecosystem provides both pretrained models and tools for training custom NER systems.

Sentiment analysis and text classification are well supported in Julia. The ecosystem includes implementations of various classification algorithms specifically optimized for text data. These can be combined with Julia's machine learning packages to create sophisticated text analysis pipelines.

Topic modeling and document clustering capabilities are provided through packages that implement algorithms like Latent Dirichlet Allocation (LDA) and Non negative Matrix Factorization (NMF). These implementations are efficient and can handle large document collections while providing intuitive interfaces for model parameter tuning.

Word embeddings and vector representations of text are supported through various packages in the Julia ecosystem. This includes implementations of popular embedding algorithms like Word2Vec and GloVe, as well as tools for working with pretrained embeddings. The ecosystem provides efficient methods for training and using these representations in downstream tasks.

Text similarity measures and distance metrics specific to text data are implemented efficiently in Julia. These include string distance measures, semantic similarity metrics, and document comparison methods. The implementations take advantage of Julia's type system and multiple dispatch to provide both flexibility and performance.

Information extraction from text is supported through various tools in the ecosystem. This includes regular expression based extractors, pattern matching systems, and more sophisticated approaches using machine learning. The ecosystem provides capabilities for extracting structured information from unstructured text data.

Text summarization capabilities are available through packages that implement both extractive and abstractive summarization approaches. These implementations leverage Julia's computational efficiency while providing high level interfaces for controlling summarization parameters and output.

Integration with deep learning frameworks is seamless for text processing tasks. Packages like Flux.jl can be used to implement neural network architectures specific to NLP tasks, such as recurrent neural networks and transformers. The ecosystem supports both training new models and using pretrained language models.

Working with large text datasets requires efficient processing strategies. Julia provides tools for streaming text processing, memory efficient operations, and distributed computing approaches specific to text data. These capabilities enable processing of large scale text collections while maintaining good performance.

Text visualization tools are available in the ecosystem, including word clouds, term frequency visualizations, and network representations of text relationships. These visualization capabilities integrate well with Julia's general purpose plotting libraries and provide insights into text data characteristics.

Integration with external NLP libraries is possible through Julia's foreign function interface. This allows Julia programs to leverage existing Python NLP libraries while maintaining the advantages of Julia's native ecosystem. The integration capabilities enable use of popular tools like spaCy and NLTK within Julia applications.

Production deployment of text processing pipelines requires consideration of performance, scalability, and integration with other systems. Julia's ecosystem provides tools for building efficient, maintainable text processing applications that can handle large volumes of text data effectively.

The text processing and NLP ecosystem in Julia continues to evolve with new packages and capabilities being added regularly. This includes specialized packages for specific domains such as biomedical text processing or legal document analysis. The ecosystem maintains a balance between providing high level abstractions for common tasks while allowing fine grained control when needed.

Chapter 19: Graph Analytics

Graph analytics in Julia provides powerful tools for analyzing and manipulating network structures through packages like Graphs.jl, NetworkLayout.jl, and GraphPlot.jl. These packages offer comprehensive functionality for working with various types of graphs, from simple undirected graphs to complex weighted and directed networks.

Graphs.jl serves as the foundational package for graph analytics in Julia. It provides efficient implementations of graph data structures and fundamental algorithms. The package supports both directed and undirected graphs, allows for vertex and edge attributes, and implements a wide range of graph operations through an intuitive interface that leverages Julia's multiple dispatch system.

Creating graphs in Julia is straightforward, with multiple construction methods available. Graphs can be built from edge lists, adjacency matrices, or incrementally through vertex and edge addition. The package supports various graph types including simple graphs, directed graphs, weighted graphs, and multigraphs, making it suitable for modeling diverse network structures.

Basic graph operations are efficiently implemented in Graphs.jl. These include adding and removing vertices and edges, checking connectivity, finding neighbors, and computing basic properties like degree distributions. The implementation takes advantage of Julia's performance characteristics while providing a high level interface for graph manipulation.

Graph traversal algorithms are fundamental to network analysis, and Julia's ecosystem provides efficient implementations of both depth first search (DFS) and breadth first search (BFS). These algorithms form the basis for more complex graph operations and can be customized through Julia's multiple dispatch system to handle specific traversal requirements.

Shortest path algorithms are well supported in the ecosystem. Implementations include Dijkstra's algorithm, Floyd Warshall algorithm, and Bellman Ford algorithm. These implementations are optimized for performance and can handle both weighted and unweighted graphs while providing flexibility in specifying custom distance metrics.

Centrality measures are crucial for understanding network structure and identifying important vertices. Julia's graph packages implement various centrality metrics including degree centrality, betweenness centrality, closeness centrality, and eigenvector centrality. The implementations are efficient and can handle large networks while providing options for parallelization.

Community detection algorithms are available for identifying groups of densely connected vertices. The ecosystem includes implementations of popular community detection methods such as the Louvain algorithm, label propagation, and spectral clustering. These implementations can handle both weighted and unweighted networks while providing parameters for controlling the granularity of community structure.

Graph visualization is supported through GraphPlot.jl and its integration with Julia's plotting ecosystem. The package provides various layout algorithms including force directed layouts, circular layouts, and spectral layouts. Visualization options can be customized to highlight different aspects of graph structure and properties.

Network analysis metrics are implemented efficiently in the ecosystem. These include clustering coefficients, assortativity, graph diameter, and various other structural properties. The implementations take advantage of Julia's performance capabilities while providing intuitive interfaces for computing and analyzing these metrics.

Random graph generation is supported through various models including Erdős Rényi graphs, Watts Strogatz small world networks, and Barabási Albert scale free networks. These implementations allow for generating synthetic networks with specific properties for testing and analysis purposes.

Graph algorithms for specific applications are available through specialized packages. These include implementations for maximum flow problems, minimum spanning trees, graph coloring, and isomorphism testing. The ecosystem provides both classical algorithms and modern approaches optimized for different types of networks.

Working with large graphs requires efficient data structures and algorithms. Julia's graph packages implement memory efficient representations and provide options for handling graphs that don't fit in memory. The ecosystem includes tools for streaming graph processing and distributed graph computations.

Graph machine learning capabilities are available through integration with Julia's machine learning ecosystem. This includes implementations of graph neural networks, graph embedding methods, and algorithms for link prediction and node classification. These implementations leverage Julia's automatic differentiation and GPU support for efficient training.

Temporal and dynamic graphs are supported through specialized data structures and algorithms. The ecosystem provides tools for analyzing evolving networks, computing temporal metrics, and modeling dynamic processes on networks. These capabilities are particularly useful for analyzing time varying network data.

Integration with external graph processing libraries is possible through Julia's foreign function interface. This allows Julia programs to leverage existing graph libraries while maintaining the advantages of Julia's native ecosystem. The integration capabilities enable use of specialized graph processing tools within Julia applications.

Graph analytics in production environments requires consideration of performance, scalability, and integration with other systems. Julia's ecosystem provides tools for building efficient, maintainable graph analysis applications that can handle large scale networks effectively.

The graph analytics ecosystem in Julia continues to grow with new packages and capabilities being added regularly. This includes specialized packages for specific domains such as social network analysis, biological network analysis, or transportation network optimization. The ecosystem maintains a balance between providing high level abstractions for common tasks while allowing detailed control when needed.

Parallel and distributed graph processing is supported through Julia's parallel computing capabilities. The ecosystem includes implementations of distributed graph algorithms and provides tools for processing large graphs across multiple machines while maintaining good performance characteristics.

Graph databases can be integrated with Julia's graph processing capabilities through database connectivity packages. This enables working with persistent graph storage while leveraging Julia's in memory graph processing capabilities for analysis and computation.

Chapter 20: Differential Equations

Differential equations form a cornerstone of scientific computing and mathematical modeling, and Julia provides powerful tools for solving these equations through packages like DifferentialEquations.jl. This comprehensive ecosystem offers state of the art solvers and tools for ordinary differential equations (ODEs), stochastic differential equations (SDEs), delay differential equations (DDEs), and partial differential equations (PDEs).

The DifferentialEquations.jl package serves as the foundation for differential equation solving in Julia. It provides a unified interface for defining and solving various types of differential equations while maintaining excellent performance characteristics. The package leverages Julia's multiple dispatch system to automatically select appropriate solution methods based on the problem structure.

Defining ordinary differential equations in Julia is straightforward and intuitive. Users can specify the system dynamics through functions that describe the derivatives, with optional parameters and initial conditions. The syntax closely mirrors mathematical notation, making it easy to translate mathematical models into code while maintaining readability and correctness.

The solver ecosystem includes a wide range of numerical methods for ODEs. These include explicit methods like Runge Kutta schemes, implicit methods for stiff equations, and specialized solvers for specific problem types. The implementation automatically handles adaptive time stepping and error control while providing options for fine tuning solver behavior.

Stochastic differential equations require specialized numerical methods, and Julia's ecosystem provides comprehensive support for these problems. The available solvers include both strong and weak approximation methods, with implementations of various schemes like Euler Maruyama, Milstein, and stochastic Runge Kutta methods. The framework handles both additive and multiplicative noise terms efficiently.

Delay differential equations present unique challenges for numerical solution, and Julia's ecosystem includes specialized solvers for these problems. The implementation handles both constant and state dependent delays, with methods that maintain accuracy and stability while dealing with the historical state requirements of delay equations.

Partial differential equations can be solved through various approaches in Julia. The ecosystem supports method of lines transformations, finite difference methods, finite element methods, and spectral methods. These implementations leverage Julia's array operations and automatic differentiation capabilities for efficient solution of PDE systems.

Boundary value problems require different solution approaches compared to initial value problems, and Julia's ecosystem provides specialized solvers for these cases. The implementation includes shooting methods, finite difference methods, and collocation methods for solving boundary value problems while maintaining good convergence properties.

Performance optimization for differential equation solving is handled automatically by the ecosystem. The implementation includes automatic stiffness detection, sophisticated time stepping strategies, and efficient memory management. Users can also fine tune performance through various solver options and specialized methods for specific problem types.

The callback system in DifferentialEquations.jl provides powerful tools for controlling solution behavior. Users can define events that trigger specific actions, implement complex termination conditions, or modify the system state during integration. This flexibility allows handling complex modeling requirements while maintaining solution accuracy.

Parameter estimation and sensitivity analysis are well supported in the ecosystem. The implementation includes tools for computing parameter sensitivities through various methods including forward sensitivity analysis and adjoint methods. These capabilities integrate well with Julia's optimization packages for parameter fitting applications.

Uncertainty quantification in differential equation solutions is supported through various tools. The ecosystem includes methods for probability space discretization, Monte Carlo analysis, and polynomial chaos expansions. These implementations allow quantifying the impact of parameter and initial condition uncertainties on solution behavior.

High dimensional differential equations present computational challenges that Julia's ecosystem addresses through various specialized methods. The implementation includes tools for dealing with large systems efficiently, with support for sparse matrices and specialized solvers for high dimensional problems.

GPU acceleration is available for certain types of differential equation problems through CUDA.jl integration. The implementation includes GPU enabled solvers that can significantly accelerate solution of suitable problems while maintaining the same high level interface as CPU based solvers.

Integration with Julia's machine learning ecosystem enables solving differential equations within neural networks and other machine learning models. This includes implementations of neural differential equations and physics informed neural networks that combine differential equation solving with machine learning approaches.

The modeling interface in DifferentialEquations.jl supports composition of complex systems. Users can build models from components, combine different types of equations, and specify interactions between subsystems. This modularity facilitates building and maintaining complex models while ensuring efficient solution.

Visualization of differential equation solutions is supported through integration with Julia's plotting ecosystem. The implementation provides tools for plotting solution trajectories, phase space representations, and parameter dependence studies. These visualization capabilities help in understanding solution behavior and debugging models.

Working with differential equations in production environments requires consideration of reliability and performance. Julia's ecosystem provides tools for building robust differential equation solvers that can handle various edge cases while maintaining good performance characteristics. The implementation includes extensive testing and validation capabilities to ensure solution reliability.

The differential equations ecosystem in Julia continues to evolve with new methods and capabilities being added regularly. This includes implementations of novel numerical schemes, specialized solvers for specific problem classes, and tools for handling increasingly complex modeling requirements. The ecosystem maintains a balance between providing cutting edge capabilities and ensuring stability and reliability for production use.

Parallel computing capabilities are available for certain types of differential equation problems. The implementation includes parallel time stepping methods, parallel ensemble methods for uncertainty quantification, and distributed computing options for large scale problems. These capabilities enable efficient solution of computationally demanding problems while leveraging available computing resources.

Chapter 21: Numerical Integration

Numerical integration forms a fundamental component of scientific computing and data analysis, with applications ranging from simple area calculations to complex physical simulations. Julia provides several powerful packages and methods for handling numerical integration tasks efficiently and accurately.

The QuadGK.jl package serves as the primary tool for general purpose numerical integration in Julia, implementing adaptive Gauss Kronrod quadrature methods. This approach provides an excellent balance between accuracy and computational efficiency for many common integration problems. The package automatically handles error estimation and adaptive refinement of the integration grid to achieve specified tolerance levels.

For basic integration tasks, the implementation is straightforward. Users can define their integrand as a function and specify the integration limits. The package handles both finite and infinite intervals, with automatic transformation of improper integrals to ensure reliable results. The interface supports both real and complex valued functions, making it versatile for various applications.

Multiple integration presents additional challenges, and Julia provides several approaches for handling these cases. The Cuba.jl package implements various algorithms for multidimensional integration, including deterministic and Monte Carlo methods. These implementations efficiently handle higher dimensional problems while providing error estimates and adaptive sampling strategies.

Singular integrals require special treatment, and Julia's ecosystem includes methods for handling various types of singularities. The implementation can deal with endpoint singularities, interior singularities, and oscillatory integrands through specialized quadrature rules and transformation techniques. This capability is crucial for many physical applications where singularities naturally arise.

The HCubature.jl package provides methods specifically designed for high dimensional integration problems. The implementation uses adaptive algorithms that can efficiently handle integrands in many dimensions, with automatic error estimation and convergence monitoring. The package includes both deterministic and probabilistic methods for different types of problems.

Integration over irregular domains is supported through various techniques. The implementation can handle complex geometries through domain transformation methods, boundary representation approaches, and specialized quadrature rules. This flexibility allows accurate integration over non rectangular domains while maintaining computational efficiency.

Periodic integrands receive special treatment through specialized quadrature rules. The implementation includes methods optimized for periodic functions, taking advantage of their special properties to achieve better accuracy and performance. These techniques are particularly useful in signal processing and physical applications involving periodic phenomena.

The FastGaussQuadrature.jl package provides highly optimized implementations of Gaussian quadrature rules. These methods are particularly efficient for smooth integrands and can achieve high accuracy with relatively few function evaluations. The implementation includes various weight functions and can handle both standard and generalized Gaussian quadrature.

Integration of interpolated functions is well supported through specialized methods. The implementation can efficiently handle various types of interpolation, including polynomial, spline, and rational approximations. These capabilities are important when working with discretely sampled data that requires integration.

Automatic differentiation capabilities in Julia can be combined with integration methods to compute derivatives of integrals. This feature is particularly useful in optimization problems where gradients of integral quantities are needed. The implementation handles both forward and reverse mode automatic differentiation efficiently.

The ecosystem includes tools for dealing with stochastic integrals, important in financial mathematics and random process modeling. The implementation supports both Ito and Stratonovich interpretations, with methods for handling various types of noise processes and ensuring proper convergence properties.

Parallel computing capabilities are available for certain types of integration problems. The implementation can distribute integration tasks across multiple processors, particularly useful for Monte Carlo integration and other methods that can be naturally parallelized. This allows efficient utilization of available computing resources for computationally intensive problems.

Error estimation and uncertainty quantification are important aspects of numerical integration. The implementation provides various tools for assessing integration accuracy, including error bounds, convergence indicators, and sensitivity analysis capabilities. These features help ensure reliable results in practical applications.

Integration with Julia's optimization packages allows solving problems involving integral constraints or objective functions. The implementation handles these cases efficiently, providing gradient information when possible and supporting various optimization algorithms. This capability is particularly useful in optimal control and design optimization problems.

When working with experimental data, numerical integration often needs to handle noisy or incomplete information. The implementation includes methods for robust integration in the presence of noise, with options for filtering and smoothing as part of the integration process. These features help ensure reliable results when working with real world data.

The integration ecosystem in Julia continues to evolve with new methods and capabilities being added regularly. This includes implementations of novel quadrature schemes, specialized methods for particular problem classes, and tools for handling increasingly complex integration requirements. The ecosystem maintains a balance between providing cutting edge capabilities and ensuring reliability for production use.

Performance optimization for numerical integration is handled through various techniques. The implementation includes automatic method selection, adaptive refinement strategies, and efficient memory management. Users can also fine tune performance through various options and specialized methods for specific problem types.

Integration with Julia's differential equation ecosystem allows solving problems that combine integration and differential equations. This includes implementations of integral equations, integro differential equations, and various hybrid problems. The unified interface makes it straightforward to work with these complex mathematical models.

The ecosystem provides extensive documentation and testing capabilities to ensure reliable integration results in production environments. This includes validation against known analytical solutions, convergence testing, and performance benchmarking tools. These features help users develop robust and efficient integration code for practical applications.

Chapter 22: Monte Carlo Methods

Monte Carlo methods represent a powerful class of computational techniques that leverage random sampling to solve complex problems in numerical integration, optimization, and statistical inference. In Julia, these methods are particularly well supported through various packages and native language features that make implementation both efficient and straightforward.

At its core, Monte Carlo simulation relies on repeated random sampling to obtain numerical results. Julia's excellent random number generation capabilities, provided through the Random module, form the foundation for these methods. The language offers multiple random number generators with different properties, allowing users to select the most appropriate one for their specific application.

The basic Monte Carlo integration method provides an intuitive introduction to these techniques. By randomly sampling points within a domain and evaluating a function at these points, we can estimate integrals that might be difficult or impossible to compute analytically. Julia's efficient array operations and vectorization capabilities make this process particularly fast, especially for high dimensional problems where traditional quadrature methods become impractical.

Importance sampling represents a crucial variance reduction technique in Monte Carlo methods. By carefully choosing the sampling distribution to focus on regions that contribute most significantly to the final result, we can dramatically improve estimation accuracy. Julia's flexible type system and multiple dispatch make it easy to implement various importance sampling strategies while maintaining good performance.

Markov Chain Monte Carlo (MCMC) methods form a particularly important class of algorithms for sampling from complex probability distributions. The Turing.jl package provides a comprehensive framework for MCMC sampling, supporting various algorithms including Metropolis Hastings, Hamiltonian Monte Carlo, and No U Turn Sampling (NUTS). These implementations leverage Julia's type system to provide both flexibility and performance.

Particle filters and Sequential Monte Carlo methods are well supported through packages like SequentialMonteCarlo.jl. These techniques are particularly useful for state estimation in dynamic systems and online learning problems. Julia's efficient implementation of these methods makes them practical for real time applications where computational performance is critical.

Monte Carlo tree search algorithms, popular in artificial intelligence and game playing applications, can be efficiently implemented in Julia. The language's support for custom data structures and efficient memory management allows for sophisticated tree search implementations that can handle large state spaces effectively.

Quasi Monte Carlo methods, which use deterministic sequences instead of random numbers to achieve better convergence properties, are supported through various packages. These implementations often provide significant improvements over standard Monte Carlo methods for certain classes of problems, particularly in numerical integration and optimization.

Bootstrap methods, which use resampling to estimate statistical properties, are straightforward to implement in Julia. The language's efficient array operations and random number generation make bootstrap calculations fast, even for large datasets. This is particularly useful in statistical inference and uncertainty quantification.

Cross validation, while not strictly a Monte Carlo method, shares many implementation details with Monte Carlo techniques. Julia's MLJ.jl framework provides comprehensive support for cross validation in machine learning contexts, leveraging the language's parallel computing capabilities for improved performance.

Parallel Monte Carlo implementations are particularly well supported in Julia through its native parallel computing capabilities. The language makes it easy to distribute Monte Carlo simulations across multiple processors or machines, with minimal code changes required to parallelize existing sequential implementations.

Variance reduction techniques beyond importance sampling, such as control variates and antithetic variates, can be efficiently implemented in Julia. The language's multiple dispatch system allows these techniques to be implemented generically, making them easily applicable to different problem types.

Monte Carlo optimization methods, including simulated annealing and genetic algorithms, are well supported through various packages. These implementations leverage Julia's efficient numerical computing capabilities and type system to provide both flexibility and performance in solving complex optimization problems.

Rare event simulation techniques, important in reliability analysis and risk assessment, can be implemented efficiently in Julia. The language's support for multiple precision arithmetic and specialized number types helps ensure accurate results even in extreme probability scenarios.

Multilevel Monte Carlo methods, which use a hierarchy of approximations to reduce computational cost, are particularly well suited to Julia's implementation style. The language's type system and multiple dispatch make it natural to express the different levels of approximation while maintaining good performance.

Adaptive Monte Carlo methods, which modify their behavior based on intermediate results, can be implemented efficiently in Julia. The language's support for mutable state and efficient array operations makes it practical to implement sophisticated adaptive strategies.

When working with Monte Carlo methods in production environments, proper random number generator management becomes crucial. Julia provides tools for managing random number streams across parallel processes and ensuring reproducibility of results, essential features for production applications.

Error estimation and convergence monitoring in Monte Carlo methods require careful implementation. Julia's statistics packages provide various tools for assessing Monte Carlo error and monitoring convergence, helping ensure reliable results in practical applications.

Integration with other numerical methods, such as differential equations or optimization algorithms, is straightforward in Julia. The language's ecosystem provides various tools for combining Monte Carlo methods with other numerical techniques, allowing for sophisticated hybrid approaches.

Performance optimization for Monte Carlo methods often involves careful management of random number generation and memory allocation. Julia provides various tools for profiling and optimizing Monte Carlo implementations, helping achieve maximum performance in production environments.

The ecosystem continues to evolve with new Monte Carlo methods and implementations being developed regularly. This includes specialized methods for particular problem domains, improved sampling strategies, and new variance reduction techniques. The focus remains on providing both cutting edge capabilities and reliable performance for production use.

Chapter 23: Bayesian Analysis

Bayesian analysis represents a fundamental approach to statistical inference that has gained significant prominence in modern data science. Julia's ecosystem provides robust support for Bayesian methods through various packages, making it an excellent platform for implementing Bayesian analyses in production environments.

The Turing.jl package stands at the forefront of Bayesian computing in Julia, offering a probabilistic programming framework that combines flexibility with performance. It allows users to specify complex probabilistic models using familiar Julia syntax while leveraging efficient sampling algorithms under the hood. This combination of ease of use and computational efficiency makes it particularly suitable for production applications where both development speed and runtime performance matter.

Prior specification forms a crucial component of Bayesian analysis, and Julia's type system makes it straightforward to work with different types of priors. The Distributions.jl package provides a comprehensive collection of probability distributions that can be used as priors, while the multiple dispatch system allows for flexible composition of these distributions. This enables practitioners to implement sophisticated hierarchical models while maintaining code readability and performance.

Likelihood functions, another essential component of Bayesian analysis, can be efficiently implemented in Julia using its native mathematical capabilities. The language's support for automatic differentiation through packages like ForwardDiff.jl and ReverseDiff.jl makes it possible to work with complex likelihood functions while maintaining good computational performance. This is particularly important in production settings where model complexity often necessitates sophisticated likelihood specifications.

Markov Chain Monte Carlo (MCMC) methods serve as the computational backbone of many Bayesian analyses, and Julia excels in their implementation. The AdvancedHMC.jl package provides state of the art Hamiltonian Monte Carlo sampling, while Turing.jl implements various other MCMC algorithms including Metropolis Hastings and No U Turn Sampling. These implementations leverage Julia's type system and multiple dispatch to provide both flexibility and performance.

Variational inference, an alternative to MCMC for approximate Bayesian inference, is well supported through packages like VariationalInference.jl. This approach becomes particularly valuable in production settings where computational speed is critical, as it often provides faster alternatives to full MCMC sampling while maintaining reasonable accuracy.

Bayesian neural networks represent an important application area where Julia's capabilities shine. The combination of Flux.jl for deep learning and Turing.jl for Bayesian inference allows practitioners to implement sophisticated Bayesian neural networks with uncertainty quantification, a crucial feature for many production applications.

Gaussian processes, a powerful class of Bayesian models, are supported through packages like GaussianProcesses.jl. Julia's efficient linear algebra capabilities make it practical to work with larger datasets using these models, while the multiple dispatch system allows for easy implementation of different kernel functions and inference methods.

Model comparison and selection in the Bayesian framework can be implemented efficiently using various information criteria and Bayes factors. Julia's statistics packages provide tools for computing these metrics, while the language's performance characteristics make it practical to implement sophisticated model comparison procedures.

Hierarchical Bayesian models, crucial for many real world applications, can be naturally expressed and efficiently computed in Julia. The language's support for nested types and complex data structures makes it straightforward to implement hierarchical models, while its computational efficiency makes their fitting practical even for large datasets.

Bayesian optimization, combining Bayesian inference with optimization, is well supported through packages like BayesianOptimization.jl. This becomes particularly valuable in production settings for hyperparameter tuning and experimental design, where efficient exploration of parameter spaces is crucial.

Posterior predictive checks and model validation procedures can be implemented efficiently in Julia, leveraging its array operations and random number generation capabilities. These diagnostic tools are essential for ensuring model reliability in production environments, and Julia's performance characteristics make it practical to run extensive validation procedures.

Integration with external Bayesian software through interfaces like RCall.jl and PyCall.jl allows practitioners to leverage existing implementations when needed. This becomes particularly valuable in production environments where interoperability with existing workflows is important.

Computational efficiency in Bayesian analysis often requires careful attention to memory management and algorithm implementation. Julia's built in profiling tools and performance optimization capabilities make it possible to identify and resolve computational bottlenecks, ensuring efficient production deployment.

When working with large datasets, efficient data handling becomes crucial for Bayesian analysis. Julia's DataFrames.jl and other data management tools provide efficient ways to handle large datasets while maintaining good computational performance during Bayesian inference.

Parallel computation of Bayesian analyses is well supported through Julia's native parallel computing capabilities. This becomes particularly valuable when fitting multiple models or working with large datasets, allowing for efficient utilization of available computational resources.

Storage and serialization of Bayesian model results require careful consideration in production environments. Julia provides various tools for efficiently storing and loading model results, ensuring that analyses can be easily reproduced and results can be efficiently accessed when needed.

Visualization of Bayesian analysis results is well supported through packages like Plots.jl and MCMCChains.jl. These tools provide various ways to examine posterior distributions, trace plots, and other diagnostic visualizations essential for understanding and validating Bayesian analyses.

The integration of Bayesian methods into larger data science workflows is straightforward in Julia, thanks to its comprehensive ecosystem and efficient interoperability with other tools. This makes it practical to implement end to end workflows that incorporate Bayesian analysis alongside other statistical and machine learning methods.

As Bayesian methods continue to evolve, Julia's ecosystem keeps pace with new developments in the field. This includes implementation of newer sampling algorithms, more efficient computational methods, and tools for handling increasingly complex models, ensuring that practitioners have access to state of the art methods for their production applications.

Chapter 24: Distributed Computing Fundamentals

Chapter 24 focuses on distributed computing fundamentals in Julia, a critical aspect for scaling data science applications across multiple machines and processors. Julia's built-in distributed computing capabilities make it an excellent choice for handling large-scale computational tasks in production environments.

The foundation of distributed computing in Julia rests on its Distributed standard library, which provides core functionality for parallel and distributed computation. Understanding this foundation is crucial for building scalable applications. The library implements a message passing model that allows processes to communicate and coordinate their activities, enabling efficient parallel execution of computational tasks.

Julia's distributed computing model centers around the concept of remote references and remote calls. When you add multiple processes to a Julia session using addprocs(), each process runs in its own memory space, and communication between processes happens through message passing. This design choice ensures good isolation between processes and helps prevent many common concurrent programming issues.

The @everywhere macro plays a vital role in distributed computing with Julia. It allows you to define functions and variables that are available across all processes. This becomes particularly important when implementing distributed algorithms where different processes need to execute the same code. However, it's important to use @everywhere judiciously, as excessive use can impact performance and increase memory usage.

Distributed arrays form another cornerstone of Julia's distributed computing capabilities. These arrays are split across multiple processes, allowing for parallel operations on large datasets that might not fit in the memory of a single machine. The DistributedArrays.jl package provides a comprehensive implementation of distributed arrays, supporting various operations while maintaining good performance characteristics.

Remote references in Julia come in several forms, including Future and RemoteChannel. Future represents a value that will be available at some point in the future, typically the result of a computation running on another process. RemoteChannel provides a way to communicate between processes, allowing for more complex coordination patterns than simple remote procedure calls.

The @spawnat and @distributed macros provide high-level interfaces for distributed computation. @spawnat allows you to run specific computations on designated processes, while @distributed provides a convenient way to parallelize for loops across multiple processes. These tools make it straightforward to implement various parallel computing patterns while maintaining code readability.

Load balancing becomes crucial in distributed computing scenarios, and Julia provides several mechanisms for distributing work effectively across processes. The scheduling of tasks can be handled automatically by the runtime system, or you can implement custom load balancing strategies using Julia's lower-level distributed computing primitives.

Error handling in distributed computing requires special attention, as failures can occur on any process and need to be handled appropriately. Julia provides mechanisms for catching and handling errors in distributed computations, allowing for robust error recovery strategies in production environments.

Shared state management presents particular challenges in distributed computing, and Julia provides various tools for handling shared state effectively. This includes distributed dictionaries and other distributed data structures that can be accessed and modified by multiple processes while maintaining consistency.

Communication patterns in distributed computing can significantly impact performance, and Julia allows for fine-grained control over how processes communicate. This includes support for different communication topologies and the ability to optimize communication patterns for specific application requirements.

Memory management becomes more complex in distributed settings, and Julia's garbage collection works across distributed processes to ensure efficient memory usage. Understanding how memory is managed in distributed settings is crucial for building efficient applications.

Synchronization between processes often becomes necessary in distributed applications, and Julia provides various primitives for process synchronization. This includes barriers, locks, and other synchronization mechanisms that help ensure correct program behavior in distributed settings.

Performance monitoring and debugging of distributed applications present unique challenges, and Julia provides tools for understanding the behavior of distributed computations. This includes facilities for monitoring process status, tracking communication patterns, and identifying performance bottlenecks.

Integration with cluster management systems is often necessary in production environments, and Julia provides good support for running distributed computations on various cluster setups. This includes support for common job scheduling systems and cloud computing platforms.

Data locality considerations become important in distributed computing, and Julia's distributed computing model allows for control over data placement and movement. This becomes particularly important when working with large datasets where minimizing data movement can significantly impact performance.

Network configuration and security considerations play important roles in distributed computing, and Julia provides mechanisms for configuring network settings and implementing security measures in distributed applications. This includes support for encryption and authentication in process communication.

The interaction between distributed computing and Julia's type system provides interesting opportunities for optimization. The multiple dispatch system can be used to implement specialized behavior for distributed types, leading to more efficient distributed computations.

Fault tolerance becomes crucial in distributed settings, and Julia provides mechanisms for handling process failures and implementing fault-tolerant algorithms. This includes support for checkpointing and recovery strategies that can help ensure reliable operation in production environments.

Resource management in distributed settings requires careful attention, and Julia provides tools for monitoring and managing resource usage across processes. This includes facilities for controlling CPU and memory usage, as well as managing other system resources.

The scalability of distributed applications depends heavily on how they're implemented, and Julia's distributed computing model provides good support for building scalable applications. This includes support for both strong and weak scaling, allowing applications to effectively utilize additional computational resources.

Chapter 25: Parallel Computing Patterns

Chapter 25 builds upon the distributed computing fundamentals covered previously to explore specific parallel computing patterns that are commonly used in production data science applications. These patterns provide structured approaches to solving parallel computation problems efficiently in Julia.

The Map-Reduce pattern stands as one of the most fundamental parallel computing patterns, and Julia provides excellent support for implementing it efficiently. In its simplest form, the pattern involves mapping a function across a collection of data in parallel, then reducing the results to a single value. Julia's pmap function provides a straightforward way to implement the map phase, while reduce handles the combination of results. This pattern proves particularly useful for data processing tasks where operations on individual elements are independent.

The Master-Worker pattern, also known as the Task Farm pattern, represents another crucial parallel computing paradigm. In this pattern, a master process distributes tasks to worker processes and coordinates their execution. Julia's remote procedure call capabilities, combined with RemoteChannel, make implementing this pattern straightforward. The master can maintain a queue of tasks and distribute them to workers as they become available, providing natural load balancing.

Pipeline parallelism represents a pattern where different stages of computation are performed by different processes, with data flowing through the pipeline. Julia's channel abstraction provides an excellent foundation for implementing pipeline parallelism. By connecting processes through channels, you can create efficient data processing pipelines where each stage operates concurrently on different data elements.

The Divide and Conquer pattern naturally lends itself to parallel implementation, and Julia's recursive task splitting capabilities make it straightforward to implement parallel versions of divide and conquer algorithms. This pattern proves particularly useful for problems that can be broken down into smaller, independent subproblems, such as sorting or tree traversal algorithms.

Data parallelism represents a fundamental pattern where the same operation is performed on different portions of data simultaneously. Julia's distributed arrays provide built-in support for data parallelism, allowing operations to be performed on different sections of an array in parallel. This pattern proves particularly useful for numerical computing and matrix operations.

The Scatter-Gather pattern involves distributing data from a single process to multiple processes (scatter), performing computations in parallel, and then collecting the results back to a single process (gather). Julia provides various mechanisms for implementing this pattern efficiently, including broadcast operations and collective communication primitives.

Event-based parallelism represents a pattern where computation is driven by the occurrence of events. Julia's event handling capabilities, combined with its distributed computing features, allow for efficient implementation of event-driven parallel systems. This pattern proves particularly useful for reactive systems and real-time data processing applications.

The Producer-Consumer pattern represents another fundamental parallel computing pattern where one or more producer processes generate data or tasks that are consumed by one or more consumer processes. Julia's Channel abstraction provides an excellent mechanism for implementing this pattern, with built-in synchronization and buffering capabilities.

Parallel reduction patterns come into play when multiple processes need to combine their results into a single value. Julia provides various reduction operations that can be performed efficiently in parallel, and the @distributed macro makes it easy to implement custom reduction operations.

The Stencil pattern, common in scientific computing, involves parallel updates to array elements based on neighboring values. Julia's array abstractions and distributed computing capabilities make it straightforward to implement efficient stencil computations in parallel.

Load balancing patterns become crucial when dealing with irregular workloads. Julia provides several approaches to load balancing, from simple round-robin distribution to more sophisticated dynamic load balancing strategies. The choice of load balancing pattern can significantly impact the performance of parallel applications.

Synchronization patterns help coordinate the activities of multiple processes. Julia provides various synchronization primitives, including barriers and locks, allowing for the implementation of different synchronization patterns. However, it's important to minimize synchronization overhead in parallel applications.

Fault tolerance patterns help ensure reliable operation in the presence of failures. Julia's distributed computing infrastructure supports various fault tolerance patterns, from simple retry mechanisms to more sophisticated checkpoint-restart approaches.

Communication patterns determine how processes exchange information. Julia supports various communication patterns, from point-to-point communication to collective operations. The choice of communication pattern can significantly impact performance, particularly in distributed settings.

State management patterns help handle shared state in parallel applications. Julia provides various mechanisms for managing shared state, from distributed data structures to more sophisticated consistency protocols.

The Observer pattern proves useful in parallel settings where multiple processes need to be notified of changes to shared state. Julia's event handling capabilities make it straightforward to implement efficient observer patterns in parallel applications.

Parallel iteration patterns provide different ways to parallelize loops and iterations. Julia's @distributed and pmap provide high-level support for parallel iteration, while lower-level primitives allow for more fine-grained control.

Resource pooling patterns help manage shared resources efficiently in parallel applications. Julia provides various mechanisms for implementing resource pools, from simple worker pools to more sophisticated resource management strategies.

Error handling patterns become particularly important in parallel applications where failures can occur on any process. Julia provides various mechanisms for handling errors in parallel settings, from simple error propagation to more sophisticated error recovery strategies.

These parallel computing patterns provide tested solutions to common parallel programming challenges. Understanding and applying these patterns effectively can significantly improve the performance and reliability of parallel applications in Julia. However, it's important to choose patterns appropriate for the specific requirements and constraints of your application.

Chapter 26: GPU Computing with CUDA.jl

GPU computing represents a powerful paradigm for accelerating data science workloads in Julia through the CUDA.jl package. This chapter explores how to leverage graphics processing units (GPUs) effectively for computational tasks that can benefit from massive parallelization.

CUDA.jl provides a comprehensive interface to NVIDIA's CUDA platform, allowing Julia programmers to harness the power of GPU computing while maintaining the language's high level expressiveness. The package offers both low level access to CUDA primitives and high level abstractions that make GPU programming more accessible to data scientists.

Getting started with GPU computing in Julia requires having CUDA capable NVIDIA hardware and the appropriate drivers installed. The CUDA.jl package handles much of the complexity of GPU setup, allowing users to focus on the computational aspects of their problems. After installing CUDA.jl, you can verify your setup using the CUDA.functional() function which returns true if everything is configured correctly.

One of the fundamental concepts in GPU computing is the distinction between host (CPU) and device (GPU) memory. CUDA.jl provides the CuArray type, which represents arrays stored on the GPU. Converting between regular Julia arrays and CuArrays is straightforward using the cu() function for host to device transfers and Array() for device to host transfers. However, it's important to minimize these transfers as they can become a performance bottleneck.

Matrix operations represent one of the most natural fits for GPU computing. CUDA.jl integrates seamlessly with Julia's linear algebra operations, automatically executing them on the GPU when working with CuArrays. This makes it particularly easy to accelerate machine learning workloads that rely heavily on matrix operations. For example, matrix multiplication, a fundamental operation in deep learning, can see orders of magnitude speedup when executed on the GPU.

CUDA kernels represent the core of GPU computing, defining the operations that will be executed in parallel across many GPU threads. CUDA.jl provides multiple ways to write kernels. The @cuda macro offers a high level approach, allowing you to write kernel functions in pure Julia syntax. These kernels are automatically compiled to GPU code. For more control, you can also write kernels using CUDA C syntax through the @ptx and @ptx_kernel macros.

Memory management becomes particularly important when working with GPUs. CUDA.jl provides several memory types including global, shared, and constant memory. Understanding these different memory types and their appropriate use cases is crucial for achieving optimal performance. The package also includes utilities for memory allocation and deallocation, though much of this is handled automatically through Julia's garbage collector.

One powerful feature of CUDA.jl is its support for custom GPU kernels with complex memory access patterns. This allows for the implementation of sophisticated algorithms that go beyond simple array operations. However, writing efficient GPU kernels requires understanding GPU architecture concepts like thread blocks, warps, and memory coalescing.

The package includes support for CUDA streams, allowing for concurrent execution of multiple kernels and asynchronous memory transfers. This can lead to significant performance improvements by overlapping computation and data transfer. The CuStream type provides the interface for working with CUDA streams in Julia.

CUDA.jl integrates well with other Julia packages in the scientific computing ecosystem. For example, it works seamlessly with Flux.jl for GPU accelerated deep learning, and with various numerical computing packages that can leverage GPU acceleration. This integration makes it possible to accelerate existing Julia code with minimal modifications.

Profiling and optimization tools are essential for GPU computing, and CUDA.jl provides several utilities for performance analysis. The NVTX interface allows for marking regions of code for profiling, while various CUDA profiling tools can be used to analyze kernel performance and memory transfer patterns.

Error handling in GPU code requires special consideration. CUDA.jl provides mechanisms for checking CUDA errors and includes helpful error messages that make debugging GPU code easier. However, debugging GPU code can still be challenging due to the parallel nature of execution and the separate memory spaces involved.

The package includes support for various CUDA libraries like cuBLAS for linear algebra, cuDNN for deep learning, and cuSOLVER for numerical solvers. These libraries provide highly optimized implementations of common operations that can be easily accessed through Julia interfaces.

When working with large datasets, it's important to consider GPU memory limitations. CUDA.jl provides utilities for managing memory efficiently, including support for memory pools and automatic memory management. However, you may need to implement your own strategies for handling datasets that exceed GPU memory capacity.

Performance optimization for GPU code often involves different considerations than CPU code. Factors like thread divergence, memory coalescing, and occupancy become important. CUDA.jl provides various tools and utilities for measuring and optimizing these aspects of GPU performance.

The future of GPU computing in Julia looks promising, with ongoing development of new features and optimizations in CUDA.jl. The package continues to evolve to support new CUDA capabilities and provide better integration with the Julia ecosystem. As GPU hardware continues to advance, the importance of GPU computing in data science workflows is likely to grow.

In conclusion, CUDA.jl provides a powerful and flexible platform for GPU computing in Julia. While mastering GPU programming requires understanding various technical concepts, the package makes it accessible to data scientists while still providing the low level control needed for maximum performance. When used appropriately, GPU computing can provide substantial speedups for many data science workloads.

Chapter 27: Memory Management and Optimization

Memory management and optimization in Julia plays a crucial role in developing efficient data science applications. While Julia's automatic memory management handles many low level details, understanding how memory works and how to optimize its usage can significantly improve application performance.

Julia employs a garbage collector (GC) that automatically manages memory allocation and deallocation. Unlike languages such as C++ where developers must explicitly manage memory, Julia's GC handles these tasks automatically. However, this convenience doesn't mean developers can ignore memory management entirely. Understanding memory patterns and optimization techniques remains essential for writing performant code.

Memory allocation in Julia occurs when creating new objects, arrays, or data structures. Each allocation requires system resources and can impact performance, especially in tight loops or performance critical sections. One key optimization strategy involves minimizing allocations in hot code paths. This can be achieved through various techniques such as pre allocation of arrays, using views instead of copies, and employing in place operations where possible.

Pre allocation represents one of the most important memory optimization techniques in Julia. Instead of allowing arrays to grow dynamically, which requires frequent reallocation and copying, pre allocating the necessary space upfront can significantly improve performance. For example, when performing operations that build up results iteratively, pre allocating the result array can avoid repeated allocations and copies.

Memory profiling tools in Julia help identify allocation patterns and potential optimization opportunities. The @time and @allocated macros provide basic information about memory usage and allocation counts. For more detailed analysis, the Profile module includes memory profiling capabilities that can track allocations to specific lines of code. This information proves invaluable when optimizing memory intensive applications.

Type stability represents another crucial aspect of memory optimization in Julia. When the compiler can determine the exact types of variables at compile time, it can generate more efficient code and often reduce memory allocations. Using concrete types, avoiding type instabilities in functions, and ensuring type stability in hot loops can lead to significant performance improvements.

The concept of memory locality also plays an important role in optimization. Julia arrays are stored in column major order, meaning that iterating over arrays column wise generally provides better performance than row wise iteration due to CPU cache utilization. Understanding and leveraging these memory layout patterns can improve performance in numerical computations.

Memory fragmentation can become an issue in long running applications. While Julia's GC handles most fragmentation issues, some patterns can lead to suboptimal memory usage. Avoiding patterns that create many small, long lived allocations and being mindful of object lifetimes can help reduce fragmentation.

Julia provides several specialized array types that can help optimize memory usage for specific use cases. For example, StaticArrays.jl offers stack allocated arrays for small, fixed size arrays, while StructArrays.jl provides memory efficient storage for arrays of structures. Choosing the appropriate array type for your use case can lead to better memory utilization and performance.

Memory mapping through Julia's mmap functionality offers a way to work with large datasets that exceed available RAM. This technique allows files to be treated as arrays, with the operating system handling the details of loading data into memory as needed. While not as fast as working with in memory data, memory mapping provides a practical solution for working with very large datasets.

Understanding Julia's object representation and memory layout can help in optimizing data structures. For example, using immutable structures (with the immutable keyword) instead of mutable ones can lead to more efficient memory usage in certain cases. Similarly, using parametric types effectively can reduce memory overhead.

Memory pooling represents another optimization technique, particularly useful in applications that frequently allocate and deallocate objects of similar sizes. While Julia's GC handles most memory management efficiently, implementing custom memory pools for specific use cases can sometimes provide performance benefits.

Working with external libraries and interfaces requires special attention to memory management. Julia provides various tools for managing memory when interfacing with C and Fortran code, including pointer manipulation functions and utilities for managing foreign memory. Understanding these tools becomes crucial when developing applications that interface with external libraries.

The handling of temporary objects and intermediate results requires careful consideration in performance critical code. Operations that create temporary arrays can lead to unnecessary allocations. Using broadcast operations with dot syntax, fusing operations, and employing views instead of copies can help reduce these temporary allocations.

Memory bounds checking, while important for safety, can impact performance in tight loops. Julia allows bounds checking to be disabled selectively using the @inbounds macro. However, this optimization should be used judiciously and only after ensuring the code is correct, as it removes an important safety feature.

Multithreaded applications introduce additional memory management considerations. Each thread maintains its own garbage collection domain, and understanding how memory is shared and synchronized between threads becomes important for writing efficient parallel code. Proper use of atomic operations and synchronization primitives helps ensure correct memory handling in multithreaded contexts.

Memory profiling in production environments requires careful consideration. While detailed profiling can provide valuable insights, it can also impact performance. Julia provides various levels of profiling granularity, allowing developers to balance the need for information against performance impact.

The interaction between memory management and the operating system also deserves attention. Understanding how Julia's memory allocator interacts with the system allocator, how memory is mapped to physical RAM, and how virtual memory is utilized can help in optimizing applications for specific deployment environments.

Large scale data processing often requires careful memory management strategies. Techniques such as processing data in chunks, using memory mapped files, and implementing custom memory management schemes may be necessary when working with datasets that approach or exceed available RAM.

Finally, maintaining good memory management practices throughout the development lifecycle remains crucial. This includes regular profiling, monitoring memory usage patterns, and refactoring code to improve memory utilization when necessary. While Julia's automatic memory management handles many details, developers who understand and optimize memory usage can create more efficient and scalable applications.

Chapter 28: Performance Profiling

Performance profiling represents a critical aspect of developing efficient Julia applications, providing insights into code behavior and identifying optimization opportunities. Profiling tools in Julia help developers understand where their programs spend time and resources, enabling data-driven optimization decisions.

Julia provides several built-in profiling tools, with Profile.jl serving as the primary profiling framework. The @profile macro enables sampling-based profiling, collecting stack traces at regular intervals to build a statistical picture of code execution. This sampling approach introduces minimal overhead while providing valuable insights into program behavior.

Statistical profiling works by periodically interrupting the program to record the current execution state. The resulting profile data shows which functions consume the most execution time, helping developers focus optimization efforts where they'll have the greatest impact. The ProfileView.jl package provides visualization tools for this data, generating flame graphs that make it easy to identify performance bottlenecks visually.

Beyond basic timing information, Julia's profiling tools can track various performance metrics. The @time macro provides simple timing and memory allocation information, while BenchmarkTools.jl offers more sophisticated benchmarking capabilities. These tools help developers understand both execution time and resource utilization patterns.

CPU profiling reveals how programs utilize processor resources. The Profile module can track CPU time across different threads, helping developers optimize parallel code. Understanding CPU usage patterns becomes particularly important in numerical computing applications where processor utilization significantly impacts performance.

Memory profiling capabilities help track allocation patterns and identify memory-intensive operations. The @allocated macro shows memory allocation statistics, while more detailed memory profiling tools can track individual allocations to specific code locations. This information proves invaluable when optimizing memory-intensive applications.

Profile guided optimization represents an advanced technique where profiling data informs compiler optimizations. While Julia doesn't currently support automatic profile guided optimization, developers can use profiling information to manually optimize code paths identified as performance critical.

Profiling multithreaded applications requires special consideration. Julia's profiling tools support thread-aware profiling, helping developers understand how work distributes across threads and identify synchronization bottlenecks. This capability proves essential when optimizing parallel applications.

Continuous profiling in production environments helps identify performance issues that may not appear during development. While full profiling might introduce too much overhead for production use, lightweight profiling techniques can provide valuable insights without significantly impacting performance.

The StatProfilerHTML.jl package generates interactive HTML reports from profiling data, making it easier to analyze and share profiling results. These reports include detailed timing information, call graphs, and source code annotations, providing comprehensive performance insights.

Profiling specific code sections allows developers to focus on particular areas of interest. The @profile macro can target specific functions or code blocks, while custom profiling annotations can track application-specific metrics. This selective profiling helps maintain focus on relevant performance aspects.

Call graphs generated from profiling data visualize function call relationships and their associated costs. Tools like ProfileView.jl can generate interactive call graphs, helping developers understand program flow and identify optimization opportunities in the call hierarchy.

Sampling frequency configuration affects profiling accuracy and overhead. Higher sampling rates provide more detailed information but increase overhead, while lower rates reduce impact but might miss short-lived events. Choosing appropriate sampling parameters depends on specific profiling needs.

External tool integration extends Julia's profiling capabilities. Tools like Intel VTune can provide hardware-level insights, while system profilers can track operating system interactions. Combining these tools with Julia's built-in profiling provides comprehensive performance understanding.

Performance counters access enables tracking of low-level CPU events. While Julia's profiling tools don't directly expose hardware counters, packages exist for accessing these metrics. This capability helps developers understand how their code interacts with CPU features.

Profiling I/O operations helps optimize data-intensive applications. Tools for tracking file operations, network activity, and database interactions help identify bottlenecks in data processing pipelines. Understanding I/O patterns proves crucial for optimizing data science workflows.

Custom metric tracking allows developers to profile application-specific performance aspects. By implementing custom profiling hooks, developers can track domain-specific metrics alongside standard performance measurements. This flexibility helps adapt profiling to specific application needs.

Time resolution considerations affect profiling accuracy. While microsecond resolution suffices for many applications, some scenarios require nanosecond precision. Julia provides various timing functions with different precision levels to meet diverse profiling needs.

Profile data analysis requires understanding statistical implications. Since sampling-based profiling provides statistical approximations, developers must consider confidence intervals and sampling errors when interpreting results. Statistical analysis tools help extract meaningful insights from profiling data.

Profiling overhead management ensures that profiling itself doesn't significantly impact the behavior being measured. Julia's sampling-based profiler introduces minimal overhead, but developers should still consider the impact when designing profiling strategies.

Production deployment considerations influence profiling strategies. While development environments might employ comprehensive profiling, production systems typically require more selective approaches. Implementing appropriate profiling strategies for different environments helps balance insight gathering with performance impact.

Profile data storage and analysis infrastructure supports long-term performance monitoring. Tools for collecting, storing, and analyzing profiling data over time help track performance trends and identify gradual degradation. This infrastructure proves valuable for maintaining application performance.

Finally, establishing systematic profiling practices helps maintain consistent performance optimization efforts. Regular profiling, performance regression testing, and profile-driven optimization become integral parts of the development process. These practices help ensure sustained application performance as codebases evolve.

Chapter 29: Code Optimization Techniques

Code optimization techniques in Julia build upon profiling insights to enhance application performance through systematic improvements. Understanding and applying these techniques enables developers to create efficient, production-ready applications that fully leverage Julia's performance capabilities.

Type stability represents one of the most fundamental optimization techniques in Julia. When functions maintain consistent return types across all possible inputs, the compiler can generate highly optimized machine code. Developers can check type stability using the @code_warntype macro, which highlights potential type instabilities. Addressing these issues often involves explicitly declaring types or restructuring code to maintain type consistency throughout execution paths.

Memory allocation patterns significantly impact performance. Minimizing allocations, particularly in performance-critical loops, can dramatically improve execution speed. Techniques include pre-allocating arrays, using views instead of copies, and employing in-place operations where possible. The Base.@allocated macro helps track allocation behavior, while careful data structure selection can reduce memory churn.

Loop optimization plays a crucial role in numerical computing performance. Julia's compiler automatically vectorizes many loop operations, but developers can further optimize by ensuring loop invariants are hoisted, avoiding type instabilities within loops, and structuring loops to enable SIMD (Single Instruction Multiple Data) operations. The @simd macro explicitly requests vectorization when the compiler cannot automatically determine its safety.

Function specialization through multiple dispatch enables highly optimized code paths for specific input types. By defining specialized methods for common input types, developers can provide optimized implementations while maintaining generic fallback behavior. This approach combines performance with code reusability, a hallmark of Julia's design philosophy.

Compiler directives provide fine-grained control over optimization behavior. The @inline and @noinline macros suggest function inlining preferences to the compiler, while @fastmath enables aggressive floating-point optimizations. These directives should be used judiciously, as inappropriate use can sometimes degrade performance or affect numerical accuracy.

Data structure selection significantly impacts performance. Using appropriate container types for specific use cases can dramatically improve efficiency. For example, StaticArrays.jl provides stack-allocated fixed-size arrays, while sparse data structures can efficiently represent sparse matrices. Understanding the performance characteristics of different data structures enables informed choices.

Broadcasting optimization leverages Julia's efficient element-wise operation system. The dot syntax for broadcasting operations often generates more efficient code than explicit loops. However, developers should be aware of allocation patterns in broadcast operations and use in-place broadcasting where appropriate to minimize memory usage.

Function barriers help contain type instabilities and improve performance. By separating type-unstable operations into separate functions, developers can prevent instability propagation and enable better compiler optimization of the stable portions. This technique proves particularly valuable in numerical computing applications.

Compilation latency management becomes crucial in interactive applications. Techniques like function composition, avoiding global variables, and using precompilation can reduce time-to-first-plot and other compilation-related delays. Understanding Julia's compilation model helps developers structure code to minimize these impacts.

Cache-friendly code organization improves memory access patterns. Techniques include ensuring data locality, aligning data structures, and structuring algorithms to maximize cache utilization. While Julia's compiler handles many low-level optimizations, understanding cache behavior helps developers write more efficient high-level code.

Generic programming patterns enable high-performance abstract code. By leveraging Julia's type system and multiple dispatch, developers can write generic algorithms that compile to efficient implementations for specific types. This approach combines the flexibility of high-level programming with the performance of specialized code.

Custom number types allow domain-specific optimization. By implementing custom numeric types that match application requirements, developers can optimize both performance and memory usage. This technique proves particularly valuable in scientific computing applications with specific precision or representation requirements.

Parallel algorithm optimization extends beyond basic parallelization. Techniques include load balancing, minimizing synchronization points, and optimizing data movement between threads. Understanding parallel performance patterns helps developers achieve optimal scaling behavior.

SIMD optimization leverages CPU vector instructions for improved performance. While Julia's compiler automatically vectorizes many operations, explicit SIMD annotations and structured algorithms can enable additional vectorization opportunities. Understanding SIMD capabilities helps developers write vectorization-friendly code.

Memory layout optimization affects cache utilization and memory access patterns. Column-major versus row-major array access patterns, structure padding, and alignment considerations can significantly impact performance. Understanding these low-level details helps developers optimize memory-intensive operations.

Compilation optimization techniques leverage Julia's multiple compilation tiers. Understanding when functions get compiled and optimized helps developers structure code to maximize performance. Techniques include forcing compilation through precompilation and managing compilation triggers.

Algorithm selection and implementation significantly impact performance. Often, choosing an appropriate algorithm proves more important than low-level optimizations. Understanding algorithmic complexity and implementation trade-offs helps developers make informed decisions about implementation strategies.

These optimization techniques, when applied systematically based on profiling insights, enable developers to create high-performance Julia applications. The key lies in understanding which optimizations apply to specific situations and implementing them in a maintainable way that preserves code clarity while achieving performance goals.

Chapter 30: Benchmarking Against Python and R

Chapter 30 focuses on benchmarking Julia code against equivalent Python and R implementations, providing data scientists with concrete performance comparisons to inform language choice decisions. This critical analysis helps teams evaluate the benefits and trade-offs of transitioning existing codebases to Julia.

Benchmarking fundamentals require establishing fair comparisons between languages. When comparing Julia to Python or R, it's essential to use idiomatic code in each language rather than direct translations. This means leveraging vectorized operations in Python's NumPy and R's native vectors while using Julia's multiple dispatch and type system advantages. The BenchmarkTools.jl package provides robust benchmarking utilities in Julia, while Python's timeit and R's microbenchmark offer similar functionality.

Numerical computing comparisons often favor Julia's compiled nature. Matrix operations, linear algebra, and numerical integration typically show significant performance advantages in Julia compared to pure Python implementations. While NumPy and SciPy provide optimized C implementations that narrow this gap, Julia's ability to write high-level code that compiles to efficient machine code often results in cleaner implementations with comparable or better performance.

Machine learning workflows demonstrate interesting performance characteristics across languages. While Python's scikit-learn and R's caret packages benefit from years of optimization, Julia's MLJ.jl ecosystem shows competitive performance with more flexible dispatch patterns. Deep learning frameworks like Flux.jl compete effectively with PyTorch and TensorFlow, especially when custom layers or novel architectures are required.

Data manipulation tasks reveal nuanced performance profiles. Julia's DataFrames.jl performs admirably against Python's pandas and R's data.frames, particularly for operations that benefit from multiple dispatch. However, the mature optimization of pandas and data.table often shows through in common data wrangling operations. Understanding these trade-offs helps teams choose appropriate tools for specific workflows.

Statistical computing benchmarks often highlight Julia's combination of ease of use and performance. While R's statistical functions benefit from decades of optimization, Julia's ability to write generic, high-performance implementations often results in faster execution for custom statistical operations. Python's statsmodels package typically falls between these extremes in terms of performance.

Image processing comparisons demonstrate Julia's potential for high-performance computing. While Python's OpenCV bindings provide excellent performance, Julia's native image processing capabilities often match or exceed these speeds while providing more flexible interfaces. R's image processing capabilities typically lag behind both alternatives in performance-critical applications.

Text processing benchmarks reveal interesting patterns. While Python's string handling and regular expression engine are highly optimized, Julia's string operations often show comparable performance with more consistent behavior across different input types. R's text processing capabilities typically show lower performance but offer powerful statistical text analysis tools.

Memory usage comparisons require careful consideration. Julia's type system and multiple dispatch can result in larger compiled code sizes but often lead to more efficient runtime memory usage. Python's reference counting and R's copy-on-modify semantics can result in higher memory usage in certain scenarios, though both languages offer tools for managing memory efficiently.

Parallel computing benchmarks often favor Julia's native parallel capabilities. While Python's multiprocessing and R's parallel packages provide solid parallel computing options, Julia's built-in parallel computing features often result in simpler implementations with better scaling characteristics. This advantage becomes particularly apparent in distributed computing scenarios.

GPU computing comparisons show Julia's CUDA.jl package competing effectively with Python's CuPy and R's GPU computing options. Julia's ability to write generic code that works efficiently on both CPU and GPU often results in more maintainable codebases while maintaining competitive performance.

Start-up time comparisons typically favor Python and R for small scripts. Julia's just-in-time compilation introduces initial latency, though tools like PackageCompiler.jl can mitigate this for production deployments. Understanding these trade-offs helps teams design appropriate development and deployment workflows.

Integration scenarios often require careful benchmarking. While Julia can call Python and R code through PyCall.jl and RCall.jl respectively, these interfaces introduce overhead. Benchmarking these integration points helps teams decide when to reimplement functionality in Julia versus maintaining existing code in other languages.

Web service performance comparisons show Julia's HTTP.jl and web frameworks competing effectively with Python's Flask/Django and R's Plumber. Julia's efficient request handling and data processing capabilities often result in higher throughput for data-intensive web services.

Database interaction benchmarks typically show comparable performance across languages when using optimized database drivers. Julia's database interfaces often provide more type-safe queries with minimal performance overhead compared to Python's SQLAlchemy or R's DBI packages.

Real-time processing comparisons often favor Julia's combination of high performance and dynamic programming features. While Python's async capabilities and R's streaming data tools provide solid options, Julia's ability to write high-performance asynchronous code often results in more efficient real-time processing systems.

Benchmarking methodology requires careful attention to ensure fair comparisons. Factors like warm-up time, garbage collection, and system load can significantly impact results. Using standardized benchmarking suites and statistical analysis of results helps ensure meaningful comparisons across languages.

Documentation of benchmarking results should include detailed information about hardware configurations, software versions, and methodology. This enables others to reproduce results and understand how they might translate to different environments. Regular benchmark updates as languages and packages evolve help maintain accurate performance comparisons.

These benchmarking insights help teams make informed decisions about language choice for specific applications. While Julia often shows superior performance for numerical and scientific computing workloads, the mature ecosystems of Python and R provide compelling advantages for many data science workflows. Understanding these trade-offs enables teams to choose the right tool for each task while leveraging Julia's strengths where they provide the most benefit.

Chapter 31: Package Development

Package development in Julia represents a crucial skill for data scientists looking to contribute to the ecosystem and create reusable, maintainable code. The Julia package manager, Pkg, provides robust tools for creating, testing, and publishing packages that can be shared with the broader community.

Creating a new package begins with understanding Julia's package structure. The package generator utility, available through Pkg.generate(), creates a standard package template with the necessary files and directory structure. This includes a Project.toml file that specifies package metadata and dependencies, a src directory for source code, and a test directory for unit tests. This standardized structure promotes consistency across the ecosystem and makes it easier for others to understand and contribute to your package.

The Project.toml file serves as the package manifest, defining package metadata, version information, and dependencies. Managing dependencies requires careful consideration of version compatibility and the potential impact on users' environments. Julia's semantic versioning system helps developers communicate changes effectively, with major version numbers indicating breaking changes, minor versions for new features, and patch versions for bug fixes.

Package development workflows typically involve creating a development environment using Pkg.develop(). This allows you to make changes to the package while testing it in the context of a larger project. The package manager's environments feature enables isolated testing and development, preventing conflicts between different projects' dependencies.

Organizing code within a package requires thoughtful structure. The main module, defined in src/PackageName.jl, should export only the functions and types that form the package's public interface. Internal functionality should remain unexported, allowing for future refactoring without breaking downstream code. Using submodules can help organize related functionality and manage code complexity in larger packages.

Type system integration plays a crucial role in package development. Julia's multiple dispatch system enables powerful generic programming patterns, but requires careful consideration of type parameters and constraints. Abstract types should be used to define interfaces, while concrete types implement specific functionality. This approach promotes code reuse and enables users to extend package functionality through type hierarchies.

Documentation generation in Julia packages typically uses Documenter.jl, which processes docstrings and markdown files to create comprehensive package documentation. Good documentation includes detailed function descriptions, type specifications, examples, and tutorials. The @docs macro allows automatic inclusion of docstrings in generated documentation, while custom pages can provide additional context and usage guidance.

Testing infrastructure is essential for package reliability. The Test standard library provides a robust framework for unit testing, while test sets help organize related tests. Coverage tools identify untested code paths, helping developers ensure comprehensive test coverage. Continuous integration services like GitHub Actions can automatically run tests across multiple Julia versions and operating systems.

Performance considerations should guide package design from the start. Type stability, avoiding global variables, and proper function barriers help ensure efficient compilation. The @code_warntype macro helps identify potential type instability issues, while benchmarking tools measure performance impact of implementation choices. Performance critical sections may require careful optimization, possibly using lower-level programming constructs.

Error handling strategies in packages should provide meaningful error messages and appropriate error types. Custom error types help users handle specific error conditions, while error messages should provide clear guidance for resolution. The @assert macro can help validate function arguments and internal state, while try-catch blocks manage exceptional conditions.

Dependency management requires careful consideration of compatibility and maintenance burden. Minimizing dependencies reduces potential conflicts and maintenance overhead, while choosing stable, well-maintained dependencies improves package reliability. The [compat] section in Project.toml specifies version compatibility requirements, helping users avoid version conflicts.

Publishing packages to Julia's general registry involves submitting a pull request to JuliaRegistries/General. This process includes automated checks for package structure, documentation, and test coverage. Version tagging follows semantic versioning principles, with new versions requiring explicit registration. The registration process helps maintain ecosystem quality and compatibility.

Community engagement forms an important aspect of package development. Responding to issues, reviewing pull requests, and participating in discussions helps build a supportive user community. Clear contribution guidelines and code of conduct documents help manage community interactions and set expectations for contributors.

Integration with other packages requires careful design of extension points. Abstract types and multiple dispatch enable other packages to extend functionality without requiring explicit dependencies. The Requires.jl package enables optional dependencies, allowing packages to provide additional functionality when specific packages are available.

Package maintenance involves regular updates to maintain compatibility with new Julia versions and dependent packages. Deprecation warnings help users adapt to interface changes, while changelog entries document modifications between versions. Regular testing against development versions of Julia helps identify potential compatibility issues early.

Security considerations in package development include careful handling of user input, proper encryption of sensitive data, and secure network communications. Dependencies should be regularly updated to address security vulnerabilities, while security advisories communicate known issues to users.

Binary dependencies require special handling through BinaryBuilder.jl, which creates portable binary artifacts for different platforms. This enables packages to include compiled dependencies while maintaining cross-platform compatibility. The artifacts system manages binary artifact distribution and installation.

Performance profiling tools help optimize package functionality. The Profile module and ProfileView.jl provide insights into code execution patterns, while BenchmarkTools.jl enables precise performance measurements. Regular performance testing helps identify regressions and optimization opportunities.

Internationalization support enables packages to reach broader audiences. Using abstract string types and locale-aware formatting helps packages work correctly across different languages and regions. Translation frameworks can provide localized versions of documentation and error messages.

Package evolution requires careful management of breaking changes and deprecations. Major version bumps should coincide with interface changes, while deprecation warnings help users adapt to upcoming modifications. Migration guides help users update their code to work with new package versions.

The Julia package ecosystem continues to evolve, with new tools and best practices emerging regularly. Staying engaged with the community through forums, conferences, and social media helps package developers adapt to changing requirements and opportunities.

Regular review of package usage patterns and user feedback guides future development directions.

Chapter 32: Testing and CI/CD

Testing and continuous integration/continuous deployment (CI/CD) practices are essential components of modern software development, ensuring code quality and reliability in Julia packages and applications. A comprehensive testing strategy combined with automated CI/CD pipelines helps catch bugs early, maintains code quality, and streamlines the deployment process.

Julia's built in testing framework provides a robust foundation for unit testing through the Test module. The framework supports a variety of assertion types, test sets for organizing related tests, and detailed failure reporting. Basic test assertions include @test for boolean conditions, @test_throws for exception checking, and @test_approx_eq for comparing floating point values within specified tolerances.

Writing effective tests requires careful consideration of test coverage and edge cases. Unit tests should verify individual function behaviors, while integration tests ensure components work together correctly. Property based testing, available through packages like QuickCheck.jl, generates random test cases to identify edge cases and unexpected behaviors. Test parameterization allows running the same test logic with different inputs, reducing code duplication and improving coverage.

Test organization plays a crucial role in maintainability. Test sets group related tests, making it easier to understand test failures and maintain test suites. The @testset macro creates hierarchical test organizations, with nested test sets providing fine grained organization. Test fixtures setup and teardown common test requirements, while shared test utilities reduce code duplication across test cases.

Code coverage tools measure test effectiveness by tracking which code paths are exercised during testing. Coverage.jl integrates with

Julia's testing framework to generate coverage reports, identifying untested code sections. Regular coverage monitoring helps maintain and improve test quality over time. Coverage reports can be automatically generated and published as part of the CI process.

Continuous Integration automates test execution and validation processes. GitHub Actions provides powerful CI capabilities for Julia projects, with predefined workflows for common testing scenarios. CI configurations typically include testing across multiple Julia versions, operating systems, and hardware architectures. The julia-actions/setup-julia action simplifies Julia environment setup in CI workflows.

CI workflows should include both test execution and additional validation steps. Static code analysis tools can identify potential issues before runtime, while style checkers ensure consistent code formatting. Documentation generation and validation ensure documentation stays current with code changes. Performance benchmarks in CI help identify performance regressions early.

Continuous Deployment extends automation to the release process. Release workflows can automatically create new package versions, update documentation, and publish packages to registries. Version bumping tools help maintain semantic versioning consistency, while changelog generators create release notes from commit messages. Automated deployment reduces manual errors and ensures consistent release processes.

Environment management in testing requires careful consideration. Project.toml and Manifest.toml files should be committed to version control, ensuring reproducible test environments. Test specific dependencies can be specified in a separate test/Project.toml file, preventing test dependencies from affecting package users. CI environments should mirror production configurations as closely as possible.

Test driven development (TDD) practices can improve code quality and design. Writing tests before implementation helps clarify requirements and identify design issues early. The @test_skip and @test_broken macros support incremental development by marking tests that are not yet passing. Regular test execution during development catches issues quickly and maintains development momentum.

Performance testing requires special consideration. BenchmarkTools.jl provides tools for reliable performance measurements, accounting for system variability and compilation effects. Performance test suites should include both microbenchmarks for specific operations and macrobenchmarks for typical usage patterns. CI systems can track performance metrics over time, alerting on significant regressions.

Integration testing with external services requires careful management of test dependencies. Mock objects and service virtualization help isolate tests from external dependencies, while integration test environments provide controlled testing of external interactions. Feature flags and configuration management enable flexible testing of different deployment scenarios.

Security testing should be included in CI/CD pipelines. Dependency scanning tools identify known vulnerabilities in package dependencies, while security focused static analysis can identify potential security issues in code. Regular security testing helps maintain application security over time and identifies new vulnerabilities as they emerge.

Deployment validation ensures successful application deployment. Smoke tests verify basic functionality in deployed environments, while health checks monitor ongoing application operation. Deployment rollback procedures should be automated and tested regularly. Blue green deployment strategies enable zero downtime updates while maintaining the ability to quickly revert changes.

Documentation testing ensures example code remains functional. The Documenter.jl package supports running code examples as part of the documentation build process, ensuring documentation accuracy. Code coverage tools can track documentation example coverage, helping maintain comprehensive example coverage.

Error handling testing verifies appropriate error responses and recovery procedures. Chaos engineering practices intentionally introduce failures to verify system resilience. Error injection frameworks help test error handling code paths that might be difficult to trigger naturally. Recovery procedures should be regularly tested to ensure they remain effective.

Monitoring test results over time helps identify patterns and trends. Test result aggregation tools collect and analyze test outcomes, while test timing analysis identifies slow running tests that might benefit from optimization. Historical test data helps identify flaky tests that produce inconsistent results.

Database testing requires careful management of test data and state. Database cleanup procedures ensure tests start from known states, while database migrations should be tested as part of the CI process. Test data generators create realistic test data while maintaining referential integrity and business rules.

Container testing verifies application behavior in containerized environments. Container builds should be tested as part of CI, while container security scanning identifies potential vulnerabilities. Multi container testing verifies interactions between containerized services.

Load testing validates application performance under stress. Load testing tools generate realistic traffic patterns, while performance monitoring captures detailed metrics during tests. Load test environments should mirror production configurations as closely as possible while considering cost and resource constraints.

The CI/CD pipeline itself should be tested and maintained. Pipeline testing tools verify workflow configurations, while pipeline monitoring ensures efficient resource usage. Regular pipeline maintenance keeps build times reasonable and maintains pipeline reliability.

Chapter 33: Documentation Best Practices

Documentation plays a critical role in making Julia code accessible, maintainable, and usable by others. Julia provides powerful built-in documentation tools and follows established conventions that make it easy to create comprehensive, well-organized documentation for packages and applications.

Julia's documentation system centers around docstrings, which are special string literals attached to functions, types, and modules. Docstrings support Markdown formatting, allowing rich text formatting, code examples, mathematical equations, and more. The convention is to place docstrings immediately before the object they document, using triple quotes for multi-line documentation.

Documentation should follow a consistent structure that includes a clear description of functionality, input parameters, return values, and examples. Parameter descriptions should specify types and any constraints or special values. Return value documentation should detail possible outputs and any error conditions. Examples should demonstrate typical usage patterns and important edge cases.

The Documenter.jl package provides tools for generating static documentation websites from docstrings and additional markdown files. It supports features like cross-references between documentation pages, automatic inclusion of docstrings, and verification of code examples. Documentation builds can be automated through CI/CD pipelines, ensuring documentation stays current with code changes.

Organization of documentation follows a hierarchical structure. The main README.md file provides an overview and getting started information. A docs/ directory contains additional markdown files organized by topic. The standard structure includes installation instructions, basic usage examples, API reference, and advanced topics. Navigation should be intuitive, with clear relationships between sections.

Code examples in documentation serve multiple purposes. They demonstrate correct usage, provide copy-paste ready solutions, and serve as additional tests through doctests. Examples should be complete and self-contained, including necessary import statements and setup code. Complex examples should include explanatory comments and demonstrate best practices.

API documentation requires special attention to detail. Function signatures should be complete, including type parameters and constraints. Documentation should cover both the public API and any internal functions that might be useful for package extenders. Breaking changes to the API should be clearly documented in release notes and changelog entries.

Mathematical content in documentation benefits from Julia's support for LaTeX syntax. Equations should be properly formatted and numbered when appropriate. Variable names in text should match those in equations and code examples. Complex mathematical concepts should include explanatory text and references to relevant literature.

Performance characteristics and complexity analysis should be documented when relevant. This includes computational complexity, memory usage patterns, and any performance tradeoffs or limitations. Documentation should highlight opportunities for parallelization and note any thread safety considerations.

Version specific documentation helps users understand changes and migrate between versions. Documentation should clearly indicate which Julia versions are supported and any version specific features or limitations. Breaking changes should include migration guides explaining how to update code for new versions.

Configuration and environment setup deserve thorough documentation. This includes required dependencies, environment variables, and configuration options. Documentation should cover both development and production configurations, including security considerations and recommended practices.

Error messages and debugging information help users resolve issues. Common error conditions should be documented with explanations and resolution steps. Debugging guides should cover tools and techniques for identifying and fixing problems. Performance optimization guides help users improve application performance.

Package interoperability requires careful documentation. Dependencies on other packages should be clearly specified, including version constraints and any known compatibility issues. Documentation should cover integration patterns with commonly used packages and frameworks.

Deployment documentation ensures successful production deployment. This includes system requirements, installation procedures, and configuration options. Security considerations, monitoring setup, and maintenance procedures should be thoroughly documented. Troubleshooting guides help operators resolve production issues.

Documentation for parallel and distributed features requires special attention. This includes cluster configuration, resource requirements, and communication patterns. Performance scaling characteristics and potential bottlenecks should be documented to help users plan deployments.

Contributing guidelines encourage community participation. This includes code style guidelines, pull request procedures, and issue reporting templates. Documentation should cover the development workflow, including testing requirements and documentation standards for contributions.

Interactive documentation enhances learning and exploration. Jupyter notebooks provide interactive examples that users can modify and experiment with. Live documentation servers allow users to try code examples directly in the browser. Interactive tutorials guide users through complex topics step by step.

Documentation translation supports international users. Translation workflows should be documented, including tools and procedures for maintaining translations. Machine translation can provide initial coverage, but human review ensures accuracy and natural language flow.

Search functionality helps users find relevant documentation quickly. Documentation should include appropriate metadata and keywords to improve searchability. Search index generation should be automated as part of the documentation build process.

Automated documentation validation ensures quality and accuracy. This includes spell checking, link validation, and code example testing. Documentation coverage tools help identify undocumented features and functions. Regular review processes maintain documentation quality over time.

The documentation process itself should be well documented. This includes procedures for building documentation locally, preview systems for reviewing changes, and deployment workflows. Style guides ensure consistent documentation across contributors.

Chapter 34: Error Handling and Debugging

Error handling and debugging are critical skills for developing robust Julia applications. Effective error handling ensures graceful failure modes and helps users understand and recover from issues. Julia provides comprehensive tools and patterns for both error handling and debugging that help developers create reliable production systems.

Julia's error handling system is built around exceptions, which are special types that represent error conditions. When an error occurs, Julia throws an exception that can be caught and handled by error handling code. The basic structure uses try/catch blocks to handle potential errors. The try block contains code that might fail, while the catch block handles any errors that occur.

Custom error types allow applications to represent domain specific error conditions. These should inherit from Exception or a more specific built in exception type. Custom errors should include relevant information to help diagnose and resolve the issue. Error messages should be clear and actionable, providing context about what went wrong and potential solutions.

Error handling strategies depend on the application context. In interactive applications, errors might be caught and displayed to users with helpful messages. Production services often need to log errors, notify operators, and attempt recovery procedures. Library code should generally let errors propagate to the caller while adding contextual information.

The @assert macro helps catch programming errors early by checking invariants. Assertions verify assumptions about program state and fail fast when those assumptions are violated. While assertions add runtime overhead, they are invaluable during development and testing.

In production, assertions can be selectively disabled for performance critical code paths.

Stack traces provide crucial debugging information when errors occur. Julia's stack traces show the sequence of function calls leading to an error, including function names, file locations, and line numbers. The Base.stacktrace() function can capture stack traces programmatically for logging or error reporting.

The Julia debugger (Debugger.jl) provides interactive debugging capabilities. It supports setting breakpoints, stepping through code, inspecting variables, and evaluating expressions in the current context. The @enter macro starts debugging a function call, while @run debugs an entire expression. Conditional breakpoints help focus debugging on specific conditions.

Remote debugging allows debugging Julia processes running on remote systems. This is particularly useful for debugging distributed applications or production issues. Tools like remote REPL sessions and debug servers enable connecting to running processes for inspection and debugging.

Memory related issues require specialized debugging approaches. The Base.summarysize() function helps track memory usage of objects. Memory profilers can identify memory leaks and excessive allocations. Tools like HeapProfiles.jl provide detailed memory allocation information for optimization.

Race conditions in concurrent code are particularly challenging to debug. Tools like ThreadSanitizer help detect data races and synchronization issues. Logging thread IDs and using atomic operations can help track down concurrency problems. Deterministic test frameworks help reproduce race conditions reliably.

Performance debugging focuses on identifying bottlenecks and optimization opportunities. The @time and @benchmark macros provide basic timing information. Profilers show where code spends time, helping focus optimization efforts. Memory allocation profiles highlight garbage collection pressure points.

Logging plays a crucial role in debugging production systems. Structured logging with context information helps track issues across distributed systems. Log levels control verbosity, while log filters help focus on relevant information. Log aggregation tools help correlate events across system components.

Error reporting systems collect and analyze error information from production deployments. Error aggregation helps identify patterns and common failure modes. Error frequency analysis highlights reliability issues. Error correlation helps identify root causes across system components.

Debugging distributed systems presents unique challenges. Tools like distributed logging and tracing help track requests across system boundaries. Timing analysis helps identify latency issues and bottlenecks. System wide monitoring helps correlate errors across components.

Interactive debugging sessions benefit from Julia's rich REPL environment. The help mode provides quick access to documentation. The shell mode enables system interaction during debugging. The package mode manages project dependencies and environments.

Code quality tools help prevent bugs before they reach production. Static analyzers catch common programming errors. Style checkers ensure consistent code formatting. Code coverage tools identify untested code paths. These tools integrate with development workflows through pre commit hooks and CI/CD pipelines.

Error handling patterns should be consistent across an application. Error recovery procedures should be well documented and tested. Error reporting should include sufficient context for diagnosis. Error handling code itself should be thoroughly tested to ensure correct operation during failures.

Debugging tools should be configured appropriately for different environments. Development environments might enable extensive debugging features, while production systems focus on performance and security. Configuration management ensures consistent debugging setup across environments.

Production debugging requires careful security consideration. Debug information might expose sensitive data or system details. Access controls should restrict debugging capabilities appropriately. Secure communication channels protect debugging sessions from interference.

The Julia ecosystem provides additional debugging tools for specific domains. Database query debugging helps optimize database interactions. Network protocol analyzers debug communication issues. Machine learning model debugging helps understand model behavior and performance.

Effective debugging requires systematic approaches to problem solving. This includes reproducing issues consistently, isolating root causes, and verifying fixes. Documentation should include debugging guides for common issues and troubleshooting procedures for operators.

Error handling and debugging capabilities should be considered during system design. This includes error recovery procedures, monitoring points, and debugging interfaces. Architecture decisions should consider maintainability and debuggability alongside other requirements.

Chapter 35: Logging and Monitoring

Logging and monitoring are essential components of production data science systems built with Julia. A robust logging and monitoring strategy helps track system behavior, detect issues early, and maintain reliable operations. This chapter explores comprehensive approaches to implementing logging and monitoring in Julia applications.

Julia provides a built in logging framework through the Logging standard library. This framework supports different log levels including Debug, Info, Warn, and Error. Log levels help control verbosity and filter messages based on severity. The @debug, @info, @warn, and @error macros provide convenient logging interfaces with automatic source location tracking.

Structured logging enhances log analysis by adding consistent metadata to log entries. The logging framework supports arbitrary key value pairs as metadata. Common metadata fields include timestamps, request IDs, user IDs, and component identifiers. Structured logs enable efficient filtering and aggregation in log analysis tools.

LoggingExtras.jl extends the basic logging functionality with additional features. This includes log filtering based on modules or message content, logging to multiple destinations simultaneously, and rotating log files. The package also provides convenient ways to format log messages and handle logging errors.

Monitoring requires collecting metrics about system behavior and performance. The MetricsLogger.jl package provides a foundation for metrics collection. It supports various metric types including counters, gauges, and histograms. Metrics can be tagged with dimensions for flexible aggregation and analysis.

Time series metrics are particularly important for tracking system behavior over time. Tools like TimeSeries.jl help manage and analyze time series data. Common time series metrics include request rates, error rates, response times, and resource utilization. Statistical analysis helps identify trends and anomalies.

Distributed systems require coordinated logging across components. Distributed logging solutions aggregate logs from multiple processes and machines. Log correlation helps track requests across system boundaries. Distributed tracing provides detailed visibility into request processing across components.

Performance monitoring tracks system resource utilization and efficiency. This includes CPU usage, memory allocation, garbage collection activity, and network traffic. Performance metrics help identify bottlenecks and capacity issues. Alerting on performance metrics helps prevent resource exhaustion.

Application specific metrics provide insight into business logic and domain specific behavior. For data science applications, this might include model prediction rates, feature statistics, and data quality metrics. Custom metrics help track application specific service level objectives and performance indicators.

Monitoring dashboards provide visual insight into system behavior. Plots.jl and related packages enable creating interactive dashboards. Common visualizations include time series plots, histograms, and heat maps. Dashboard layouts should highlight key metrics and support drill down analysis.

Alerting systems notify operators about potential issues. Alert rules combine metrics and thresholds to detect problems. Alert severity levels help prioritize responses. Alert routing ensures notifications reach appropriate responders. Alert aggregation prevents notification storms during system wide issues.

Log analysis tools help extract insights from log data. This includes pattern matching, frequency analysis, and anomaly detection. Log analysis helps identify error patterns, usage patterns, and potential security issues. Machine learning techniques can automate log analysis for large scale systems.

Monitoring infrastructure requires careful capacity planning. Log storage needs grow with system usage. Metric databases must handle high write rates. Query interfaces must remain responsive under load. Infrastructure scaling should account for retention requirements and query patterns.

Security monitoring tracks potential security issues. This includes authentication failures, access pattern anomalies, and resource usage spikes. Security metrics help detect potential attacks or misuse. Security logs provide audit trails for compliance requirements.

Development environments often need different logging and monitoring configurations than production. Development logging might be more verbose and include debug information. Production logging focuses on operational visibility while managing storage costs. Configuration management ensures appropriate settings across environments.

Log retention policies balance visibility needs with storage costs. Different log types might have different retention periods. Log compression reduces storage requirements. Log archival moves older logs to cheaper storage. Retention policies should comply with regulatory requirements.

Monitoring systems themselves require monitoring. This includes monitoring log collection, metric storage, and alerting systems. Monitoring system failures should be detected and addressed quickly. Redundancy helps ensure continuous monitoring coverage.

Integration with external monitoring systems extends visibility options. This includes cloud monitoring services, log aggregation services, and metrics platforms. Standard protocols like OpenTelemetry enable flexible integration. External services often provide additional analysis and visualization capabilities.

Automated testing should verify logging and monitoring functionality. Tests ensure log messages contain required information. Metric collection tests verify accuracy and performance. Integration tests verify external system connectivity. Chaos testing verifies monitoring during failure conditions.

Documentation should cover logging and monitoring configurations. This includes log formats, metric definitions, and alert rules. Runbooks should document response procedures for different alert conditions. Documentation helps operators understand and maintain monitoring systems.

The Julia ecosystem continues to evolve with new logging and monitoring capabilities. This includes improved integration with cloud platforms, enhanced visualization tools, and automated analysis features. Staying current with ecosystem developments helps leverage new monitoring capabilities effectively.

Effective logging and monitoring strategies evolve with system needs. Regular review ensures monitoring coverage remains appropriate. Feedback from operators helps improve monitoring effectiveness. Continuous improvement maintains monitoring system value over time.

Chapter 36: REST API Development

Building REST APIs in Julia enables data scientists to expose their models and analytical capabilities as web services. This chapter explores the tools and patterns for developing robust REST APIs in Julia, with a focus on production readiness and scalability.

HTTP.jl provides the foundation for HTTP server functionality in Julia. Combined with Genie.jl or other web frameworks, it enables building feature rich web APIs. These frameworks handle routing, request parsing, and response formatting while maintaining Julia's high performance characteristics.

The Genie.jl framework offers a comprehensive solution for API development. It provides a structured approach to defining routes, handling requests, and organizing application logic. Genie's routing system supports various HTTP methods including GET, POST, PUT, DELETE, and PATCH. Route parameters and query strings provide flexible request handling.

Request validation ensures API inputs meet requirements. JSON Schema validation helps enforce request structure. Parameter type checking prevents invalid inputs. Input sanitization protects against malicious requests. Validation errors should return clear error messages to help API consumers.

Response formatting standardizes API output structure. JSON is commonly used for REST APIs. The JSON.jl package efficiently handles JSON serialization and deserialization. Custom serializers handle Julia specific types. Response metadata provides context for API consumers.

Authentication and authorization protect API access. JWT tokens provide stateless authentication. Role based access control manages permissions. API keys enable service to service authentication. Rate limiting prevents API abuse. Security headers protect against common vulnerabilities.

API versioning helps manage changes while maintaining compatibility. URL versioning makes versions explicit. Content negotiation provides alternative versioning approaches. Version documentation helps clients handle changes. Deprecation notices prepare for version retirement.

Error handling ensures graceful failure responses. HTTP status codes indicate error types. Error responses include descriptive messages. Stack traces should be logged but not exposed. Error handling should be consistent across endpoints.

Middleware provides cross cutting functionality. Logging middleware tracks requests and responses. Authentication middleware validates credentials. CORS middleware enables cross origin requests. Caching middleware improves performance. Custom middleware extends functionality.

Request parsing handles various content types. JSON parsing for application/json requests. Form parsing for application/x form urlencoded. Multipart parsing for file uploads. Binary data handling for specialized formats. Content type validation ensures proper parsing.

Response caching improves API performance. Cache control headers guide client caching. Server side caching reduces computation. Cache invalidation maintains consistency. Cache strategies balance freshness and performance.

API documentation helps consumers understand endpoints. OpenAPI/Swagger specifications describe API structure. Interactive documentation enables exploration. Example requests demonstrate usage. Documentation should stay synchronized with implementation.

Testing ensures API reliability. Unit tests verify endpoint logic. Integration tests check end to end functionality. Load tests verify performance. Mocking enables isolated testing. Test coverage guides testing completeness.

Monitoring tracks API health and usage. Request logging captures usage patterns. Performance metrics track response times. Error rates indicate reliability. Usage metrics guide capacity planning. Alerting detects issues early.

Rate limiting protects API resources. Request counting tracks usage. Time window limits prevent abuse. Rate limit headers inform clients. Graduated limits support different access tiers. Override mechanisms handle special cases.

CORS configuration enables web client access. Origin validation controls access. Credential handling enables authentication. Header allowlists control exposure. Preflight handling supports complex requests.

Database integration manages persistent data. Connection pooling improves efficiency. Transaction management ensures consistency. Query optimization improves performance. Connection handling remains reliable under load.

Asynchronous processing handles time consuming operations. Background jobs prevent request blocking. Job status endpoints track progress. Webhook callbacks notify completion. Queue management handles job scheduling.

API gateway integration provides additional capabilities. Authentication consolidation simplifies security. Request routing enables scaling. Rate limiting at gateway level. Analytics collection across services.

Deployment considerations ensure reliable operation. Environment configuration management. SSL/TLS certificate handling. Load balancer integration. Container deployment support. Health check endpoints.

Performance optimization maintains responsiveness. Query optimization reduces database load. Response compression reduces bandwidth. Connection pooling improves efficiency. Caching reduces computation.

API evolution handles changing requirements. Endpoint deprecation processes. Version migration support. Client communication strategies. Breaking change management. Backward compatibility maintenance.

Documentation maintenance keeps information current. API specification updates. Example code maintenance. Change log management. Deprecation notifications. Client migration guides.

The Julia ecosystem continues expanding API development capabilities. New packages provide additional functionality. Framework improvements enhance developer experience. Integration options increase deployment flexibility. Ecosystem growth enables more sophisticated APIs.

Successful REST APIs require attention to many aspects beyond basic functionality. Security, performance, documentation, and maintainability all contribute to production readiness. Regular review and updates ensure APIs continue meeting evolving needs effectively.

Chapter 37: Database Integration

Database integration forms a crucial component of production data science applications in Julia. This chapter explores how to effectively work with various database systems while maintaining performance and reliability in production environments.

The DatabaseInterface.jl (DBI) package provides a unified interface for working with different database systems in Julia. This abstraction layer enables consistent database operations across various backends while allowing for backend specific optimizations. Common database operations like connection management, query execution, and result processing follow consistent patterns regardless of the underlying database system.

PostgreSQL integration through LibPQ.jl offers robust support for this popular database system. The package provides native Julia implementations of the PostgreSQL protocol, enabling high performance data access. Connection pooling through ConnectionPools.jl manages database connections efficiently, preventing connection exhaustion under high load. Query parameterization protects against SQL injection while improving query plan reuse.

MySQL.jl enables interaction with MySQL and MariaDB databases. The package supports both synchronous and asynchronous query execution, allowing applications to maintain responsiveness during database operations. Prepared statements improve query performance and security. Binary protocol support enables efficient data transfer between Julia and MySQL servers.

SQLite integration through SQLite.jl provides embedded database capabilities. This proves particularly useful for applications requiring local data storage or prototype development. The package supports both disk based and in memory databases. Transaction management ensures data consistency. Full text search capabilities enable efficient text based queries.

Database migrations manage schema evolution. Migrations.jl provides tools for creating and managing database schema changes. Version tracking ensures consistent schema state across environments. Migration rollback capabilities enable recovery from problematic changes. Migration generation tools simplify schema modification management.

Connection pooling optimizes database resource usage. Pool configuration balances resource utilization and availability. Connection lifecycle management handles timeouts and reconnection. Health checking ensures pool connections remain valid. Pool metrics guide capacity planning and optimization.

Query building and management tools improve code maintainability. QueryBuilders.jl enables programmatic SQL query construction. Query parameterization prevents SQL injection vulnerabilities. Query logging assists debugging and performance optimization. Query plan analysis identifies optimization opportunities.

Object Relational Mapping (ORM) through Searchlight.jl provides higher level database abstractions. Model definitions map database tables to Julia types. Relationship definitions express table associations. Query DSL enables type safe database queries. Change tracking manages model updates.

Database transactions ensure data consistency. Transaction management handles commit and rollback operations. Nested transactions support complex operations. Savepoint management enables partial rollback. Deadlock detection prevents resource contention issues.

Query optimization improves performance. Index optimization ensures efficient data access. Query plan analysis identifies performance bottlenecks. Query caching reduces database load. Batch operations improve throughput for bulk operations.

Result set handling manages memory efficiently. Lazy loading defers data retrieval until needed. Streaming results handle large data sets. Result caching improves performance for frequently accessed data. Type conversion ensures proper data representation.

Database monitoring tracks system health. Connection monitoring detects availability issues. Query performance monitoring identifies slow operations. Resource utilization tracking guides capacity planning. Error tracking enables proactive issue resolution.

Replication support enables scaling read operations. Read replica configuration distributes query load. Replica lag monitoring ensures data freshness. Query routing directs operations to appropriate servers. Failover handling maintains availability.

Sharding strategies scale write operations. Shard key selection guides data distribution. Query routing handles sharded data access. Cross shard queries maintain data consistency. Shard rebalancing handles growth.

Database backup and recovery ensures data safety. Backup scheduling manages regular backups. Point in time recovery enables precise state restoration. Backup verification ensures recovery reliability. Retention policies manage backup storage.

Security considerations protect database access. Authentication configuration controls access. Authorization management restricts operations. Encryption protects data in transit and at rest. Audit logging tracks database operations.

NoSQL database integration expands storage options. MongoDB.jl enables document database access. Cassandra.jl supports wide column storage. Redis.jl provides in memory database capabilities. Neo4j.jl enables graph database operations.

Time series database support handles temporal data. InfluxDB.jl manages time series storage. TimescaleDB integration through

PostgreSQL. Time series specific optimizations improve performance. Retention policies manage historical data.

Database testing ensures reliable operation. Test databases isolate testing environments. Fixtures manage test data. Transaction rollback maintains database state. Integration testing verifies database operations.

Error handling manages database operation failures. Connection error recovery maintains availability. Query error handling provides meaningful feedback. Retry logic handles transient failures. Error logging enables issue investigation.

Performance profiling identifies optimization opportunities. Query profiling tracks execution time. Resource utilization monitoring guides optimization. Bottleneck identification directs improvement efforts. Benchmark comparisons measure improvements.

The Julia database ecosystem continues growing with new packages and capabilities. Integration options expand database support. Performance improvements enhance efficiency. Tool development improves developer experience. Community growth strengthens ecosystem stability.

Successful database integration requires careful attention to performance, reliability, and maintainability. Regular review and updates ensure database operations continue meeting application needs effectively while maintaining security and efficiency.

Chapter 38: Docker Containerization

Chapter 38 focuses on Docker containerization for Julia applications, providing a comprehensive guide to creating efficient and portable containerized environments for production data science workflows.

Docker containerization enables consistent deployment environments across different systems, making it easier to manage dependencies and ensure reproducibility of Julia applications. Understanding container fundamentals proves essential for effective production deployment of data science solutions.

Creating Dockerfiles for Julia applications requires careful consideration of base images and dependency management. The official Julia Docker images provide a solid foundation, offering various versions and configurations. Multi stage builds optimize container size by separating build dependencies from runtime requirements. Layer optimization reduces image size and improves build efficiency.

Dependency management within containers presents unique challenges for Julia applications. Package precompilation improves startup performance but increases build time and image size. Project.toml and Manifest.toml files ensure consistent package versions across environments. Binary dependency handling requires appropriate system library inclusion.

Environment configuration management adapts application behavior across deployments. Environment variables provide runtime configuration options. Secrets management protects sensitive information. Configuration file mounting enables external configuration management. Dynamic configuration supports runtime adaptation.

Container optimization improves performance and resource utilization. Base image selection impacts container size and startup time. Layer caching speeds up builds during development. Resource constraint configuration prevents container resource exhaustion. Image security scanning identifies vulnerabilities.

Development workflows benefit from containerized environments. Docker Compose simplifies multi container development environments. Volume mounting enables rapid development iteration. Network configuration manages service communication. Development tools integration maintains productivity.

Production deployment considerations ensure reliable operation. Health check configuration monitors container status. Logging configuration enables monitoring and debugging. Resource limit configuration prevents resource exhaustion. Restart policy configuration maintains availability.

Container orchestration manages production deployments. Kubernetes integration enables scalable deployments. Service discovery manages container communication. Load balancing distributes traffic. Rolling updates maintain availability during deployment.

Security considerations protect containerized applications. User configuration prevents privilege escalation. Network security isolates containers. Volume permission management protects data access. Security scanning identifies vulnerabilities.

Performance optimization improves container efficiency. Julia precompilation reduces startup time. Package artifact caching speeds up builds. System library optimization reduces image size. Resource utilization monitoring guides optimization.

Multi container applications manage complex deployments. Container networking enables service communication. Volume sharing manages shared data. Dependency ordering ensures proper startup sequence. Resource isolation prevents interference.

Continuous integration and deployment automates container lifecycle. Automated builds ensure consistent images. Testing validates container functionality. Registry management tracks image versions. Deployment automation streamlines updates.

Monitoring and logging track container health. Log aggregation centralizes monitoring. Metric collection enables performance tracking. Alert configuration identifies issues. Debugging tools assist problem resolution.

Resource management optimizes container operation. CPU allocation controls processing resources. Memory limits prevent overflow. Storage configuration manages persistence. Network configuration controls communication.

Development best practices improve container maintainability. Base image standardization ensures consistency. Build automation improves reliability. Documentation maintains knowledge. Version control tracks changes.

Production deployment patterns guide successful implementation. Blue green deployment enables zero downtime updates. Canary deployment manages risk. Rolling deployment maintains availability. Backup strategies protect data.

Testing strategies ensure container reliability. Unit testing validates functionality. Integration testing verifies container interaction. Load testing confirms performance. Security testing identifies vulnerabilities.

Debug capabilities assist problem resolution. Interactive shell access enables investigation. Log access provides insight. Network debugging tools examine communication. Monitoring tools track performance.

Version management tracks container evolution. Image tagging identifies versions. Registry management stores images. Deployment tracking maintains state. Rollback capabilities enable recovery.

Scaling strategies handle growing demands. Horizontal scaling adds containers. Vertical scaling increases resources. Auto scaling responds to load. Load balancing distributes traffic.

Storage management handles persistent data. Volume configuration manages data persistence. Backup strategies protect data. Recovery procedures restore state. Cleanup policies manage storage.

Network configuration enables communication. Service discovery connects containers. Load balancing distributes traffic. Network security isolates communication. Performance optimization improves efficiency.

Development workflows maintain productivity. Local development environments mirror production. Testing environments validate changes. Staging environments verify deployment. Production deployment ensures reliability.

Documentation maintains operational knowledge. Configuration documentation guides setup. Operational procedures guide maintenance. Troubleshooting guides assist problem resolution. Architecture documentation explains design.

The container ecosystem continues evolving with new tools and capabilities. Integration options expand functionality. Performance improvements enhance efficiency. Tool development improves user experience. Community growth strengthens ecosystem stability.

Successful containerization requires careful attention to security, performance, and maintainability. Regular review and updates ensure containerized applications continue meeting requirements effectively while maintaining reliability and efficiency.

Chapter 39: Cloud Deployment Strategies

Here's Chapter 39 focusing on Cloud Deployment Strategies for Julia applications:

Cloud deployment strategies for Julia applications require careful consideration of architecture, scalability, and resource management to ensure optimal performance and cost effectiveness. Modern cloud platforms offer various deployment options, each with distinct advantages for different types of data science workloads.

Infrastructure as a Service (IaaS) platforms provide flexibility for Julia deployments. Virtual machines offer complete control over the environment, enabling precise configuration of compute resources, memory, and storage. Custom machine images can include precompiled Julia packages and dependencies, reducing startup time. Auto scaling groups manage resource allocation based on demand, while load balancers distribute traffic across instances.

Platform as a Service (PaaS) solutions simplify deployment by managing infrastructure details. Cloud platforms supporting buildpacks can automatically detect and configure Julia applications. Environment variables manage configuration without code changes. Automated scaling handles varying workloads, while integrated monitoring provides operational visibility. Service bindings simplify integration with managed services like databases and caching layers.

Serverless deployment enables cost effective execution of Julia functions. Function as a Service platforms support Julia through custom runtimes or containers. Cold start optimization requires careful package management and precompilation strategies. Concurrent execution handles parallel workloads efficiently. Event driven architectures enable responsive processing while minimizing resource costs.

Container orchestration platforms provide robust deployment options for containerized Julia applications. Kubernetes clusters manage container lifecycle and scaling. Helm charts standardize deployment configuration. Custom resource definitions enable Julia specific management. Service mesh implementations handle inter service communication and security.

Cloud native storage solutions manage data persistence. Object storage provides cost effective data warehousing. Block storage supports high performance computing workloads. File systems enable shared access across instances. Caching layers improve access performance while reducing storage costs.

Network configuration ensures reliable communication. Virtual private clouds isolate resources. Load balancers distribute traffic. Content delivery networks cache static assets. Virtual private networks secure remote access. DNS management simplifies service discovery.

Security implementation protects cloud resources. Identity and access management controls resource access. Network security groups filter traffic. Encryption protects data at rest and in transit. Security monitoring identifies potential threats. Compliance frameworks guide security implementation.

Cost management optimizes cloud spending. Resource tagging enables cost allocation. Auto scaling minimizes idle resources. Spot instances reduce compute costs. Reserved instances provide long term savings. Cost monitoring identifies optimization opportunities.

Monitoring and logging maintain operational visibility. Metrics collection tracks performance. Log aggregation enables troubleshooting. Alerting identifies issues. Dashboards visualize system state. Tracing helps debug distributed systems.

Disaster recovery ensures business continuity. Backup strategies protect data. Replication provides redundancy. Recovery procedures restore service. Testing validates procedures. Documentation guides recovery execution.

Continuous deployment automates updates. Pipeline configuration manages deployment stages. Testing validates changes.

Approval workflows control promotion. Rollback procedures handle issues. Monitoring confirms success.

High availability architectures maintain uptime. Multi zone deployment provides redundancy. Load balancing distributes traffic. Health checking identifies issues. Automated recovery handles failures. Documentation guides operational procedures.

Performance optimization improves efficiency. Resource sizing matches workload requirements. Caching reduces computation. Query optimization improves response time. Code optimization enhances throughput. Monitoring guides optimization efforts.

Integration patterns connect services. API gateways manage external access. Message queues handle asynchronous processing. Service discovery enables dynamic configuration. Circuit breakers prevent cascade failures.

Development workflows maintain productivity. Local development environments mirror cloud configuration. Testing environments validate changes. Staging environments verify deployment. Production deployment ensures reliability.

Configuration management maintains consistency. Environment variables provide runtime configuration. Secret management protects sensitive data. Configuration files enable external management. Version control tracks changes.

Resource management optimizes utilization. Compute allocation matches workload requirements. Memory management prevents overflow. Storage configuration handles growth. Network capacity supports communication needs.

Scaling strategies handle growing demands. Horizontal scaling adds instances. Vertical scaling increases resources. Auto scaling responds to load. Load balancing distributes traffic. Cache invalidation maintains consistency.

Security best practices protect deployments. Access control limits exposure. Network isolation prevents unauthorized access. Data encryption protects sensitive information. Security monitoring identifies threats. Compliance frameworks guide implementation.

Documentation maintains operational knowledge. Architecture documentation explains design. Configuration guides assist setup. Operational procedures guide maintenance. Troubleshooting guides assist problem resolution.

The cloud ecosystem continues evolving with new services and capabilities. Managed services simplify operations. Performance improvements enhance efficiency. Tool development improves user experience. Community growth strengthens ecosystem stability.

Successful cloud deployment requires careful attention to architecture, security, and operational efficiency. Regular review and updates ensure cloud applications continue meeting requirements effectively while maintaining reliability and cost effectiveness. Understanding different cloud deployment strategies enables optimal selection for specific use cases, ensuring successful production implementation of Julia applications in cloud environments.

Chapter 40: Production System Architecture

Chapter 40 naturally follows the cloud deployment discussion by diving into production system architecture for Julia applications:

Production system architecture for Julia applications requires careful consideration of components, interactions, and design patterns to ensure reliability, scalability, and maintainability. A well-designed architecture provides the foundation for successful production deployments while enabling future growth and adaptation.

The core architecture typically follows a layered approach, separating concerns for better maintainability. The presentation layer handles user interactions, whether through web interfaces, APIs, or command line tools. The business logic layer implements domain specific functionality using Julia's powerful computational capabilities. The data layer manages persistence and retrieval operations, often integrating with various storage systems.

Service oriented architectures enable modular development and deployment. Individual services handle specific functionality, communicating through well defined interfaces. This approach allows teams to develop and deploy components independently while maintaining system cohesion. Julia's multiple dispatch system naturally supports interface based design, making it well suited for service oriented architectures.

Microservices architectures take modularity further, breaking functionality into smaller, independently deployable units. Each microservice focuses on a specific domain capability, managing its own data and processing logic. This approach enables fine grained scaling and deployment but requires careful attention to service discovery, communication patterns, and data consistency.

Event driven architectures support reactive processing patterns. Event producers generate notifications of state changes or system activities. Event consumers process these notifications, potentially generating additional events. This pattern enables loose coupling between components while supporting complex processing workflows. Julia's asynchronous programming capabilities naturally support event driven patterns.

Data processing architectures handle large scale computation efficiently. Stream processing handles continuous data flows, enabling real time analysis and response. Batch processing manages large volume periodic processing, often for reporting or model training. Hybrid approaches combine both patterns to meet varying requirements. Julia's high performance computing capabilities support efficient implementation of these patterns.

Caching architectures improve response time and reduce system load. Local caches store frequently accessed data near computation. Distributed caches provide shared storage across services. Cache invalidation strategies maintain data consistency. Cache warming prevents performance degradation during startup. Julia's memory management system enables efficient cache implementation.

Storage architectures manage data persistence requirements. Relational databases provide structured storage with transaction support. Document stores handle semi structured data flexibly. Time series databases efficiently manage temporal data. Object storage systems handle large scale binary data. Julia's database interfaces support integration with various storage systems.

Queue based architectures manage asynchronous processing. Message queues decouple producers from consumers, enabling independent scaling. Priority queues manage processing order. Dead letter queues handle failed processing. Retry mechanisms manage transient failures. Julia's asynchronous programming support enables efficient queue processing.

Authentication and authorization architectures secure system access. Identity providers manage user authentication. Role based access control manages permissions. Token based authentication supports stateless services. Security contexts propagate authorization information. Julia's cryptography libraries support secure implementation.

Monitoring architectures maintain operational visibility. Metrics collection tracks system performance. Log aggregation enables problem investigation. Distributed tracing tracks request flow. Alerting identifies issues requiring attention. Julia's logging and instrumentation capabilities support comprehensive monitoring.

High availability architectures ensure system reliability. Redundant components prevent single points of failure. Load balancers distribute traffic across instances. Health checking identifies component issues. Automated recovery handles failures. Geographic distribution provides disaster recovery capabilities.

Scalability architectures handle growing demands. Horizontal scaling adds processing capacity through additional instances. Vertical scaling increases individual instance capabilities. Auto scaling adjusts capacity based on demand. Load balancing ensures efficient resource utilization.

Configuration management architectures maintain system settings. Environment specific configuration supports different deployment contexts. Secret management protects sensitive information. Feature flags enable controlled functionality rollout. Configuration validation ensures consistency.

Deployment architectures manage system updates. Blue green deployments enable zero downtime updates. Canary deployments validate changes with limited exposure. Rollback procedures handle deployment issues. Deployment pipelines automate the process.

Integration architectures connect system components. API gateways manage external access. Service mesh implementations handle internal communication. Circuit breakers prevent cascade failures. Retry patterns handle transient issues.

Testing architectures validate system behavior. Unit tests verify component functionality. Integration tests validate component interactions. Performance tests verify system capabilities. Chaos testing validates reliability mechanisms.

Documentation architectures maintain system knowledge. Architecture diagrams explain system structure. Interface specifications define component interactions. Operational procedures guide maintenance activities. Troubleshooting guides assist problem resolution.

Version management architectures track system evolution. Source control manages code versions. Schema management handles data structure evolution. API versioning supports client compatibility. Documentation versioning maintains accuracy.

Backup architectures protect system state. Regular backups capture system data. Point in time recovery enables state restoration. Backup validation ensures recoverability. Retention policies manage storage requirements.

The architecture must evolve as system requirements change. Regular architecture reviews identify improvement opportunities. Technology updates enable new capabilities. Performance optimization enhances efficiency. Security improvements address emerging threats.

Successful production system architecture requires careful attention to all these aspects while maintaining simplicity and manageability. Regular review and updates ensure the architecture continues meeting system requirements effectively. Understanding these architectural patterns enables successful implementation of production Julia applications.

Chapter 41: Microservices with Julia

Chapter 41 explores how to build microservices architectures using Julia, focusing on creating scalable and maintainable distributed systems.

Microservices architecture in Julia leverages the language's high performance capabilities and rich ecosystem to create modular, independently deployable services that communicate through well defined interfaces. This architectural style enables teams to develop, deploy, and scale different components of an application independently while maintaining system cohesion.

HTTP.jl serves as a foundational package for building microservices in Julia, providing both client and server capabilities. Combined with JSON.jl for data serialization, these packages enable RESTful service implementation. The basic structure of a microservice typically includes routing logic, request handlers, data validation, and response formatting. Julia's multiple dispatch system naturally supports separation of concerns and clean interface design.

Genie.jl offers a more comprehensive framework for microservices development, providing routing, middleware support, and database integration. The framework's modular design allows developers to use only needed components while maintaining flexibility. Genie's built in support for WebSockets enables real time communication between services when required.

Service discovery becomes crucial in microservices architectures. Consul.jl provides integration with HashiCorp's Consul for service registration and discovery. Services register themselves with Consul during startup, enabling other services to discover and communicate with them dynamically. This approach supports both development and production environments effectively.

Configuration management for microservices requires careful consideration. Configurations.jl helps manage service specific settings, environment variables, and secrets. Different configuration profiles support development, testing, and production environments. Distributed configuration management ensures consistent settings across service instances.

Inter service communication patterns vary based on requirements. Synchronous communication using HTTP/REST works well for simple request response patterns. Message queues like RabbitMQ, accessed through RabbitMQ.jl, enable asynchronous communication. gRPC, supported through gRPC.jl, provides efficient binary communication with strong interface contracts.

Circuit breakers prevent cascade failures in microservices architectures. CircuitBreaker.jl implements the circuit breaker pattern, automatically handling failure detection and service isolation. Retry patterns, timeouts, and fallback mechanisms ensure robust communication between services even under adverse conditions.

Data management in microservices often follows the database per service pattern. Each service maintains its own data store, accessed through packages like SQLite.jl, MySQL.jl, or MongoDB.jl. This approach ensures data independence but requires careful handling of distributed transactions and eventual consistency.

Event driven patterns often complement microservices architectures. Services publish events when state changes occur, while other services subscribe to relevant events. Kafka.jl enables integration with Apache Kafka for reliable event streaming. Event sourcing patterns capture state changes as event sequences.

Authentication and authorization require special attention in distributed systems. JSON Web Tokens (JWTs) provide a stateless mechanism for security context propagation between services. OAuth2.jl enables integration with OAuth providers for centralized authentication. Role based access control ensures appropriate authorization.

Monitoring distributed services requires comprehensive instrumentation. OpenTelemetry.jl provides distributed tracing capabilities, tracking requests across service boundaries. Metrics collection through packages like Prometheus.jl enables performance monitoring. Log aggregation ensures visibility into system behavior.

Testing microservices presents unique challenges. TestContainers.jl enables integration testing with containerized dependencies. Mock services simulate external dependencies during testing. Contract testing ensures compatible interfaces between services. Performance testing validates system behavior under load.

Deployment orchestration typically relies on container technologies. Kubernetes.jl provides programmatic access to Kubernetes clusters for service deployment and management. Docker containers package services with their dependencies. Service mesh implementations manage inter service communication and security.

Load balancing distributes traffic across service instances. Native cloud provider load balancers or solutions like HAProxy handle external traffic. Service mesh implementations manage internal load balancing. Health checking ensures traffic routes only to healthy instances.

API gateways often front microservices architectures, providing a single entry point for external clients. The gateway handles cross cutting concerns like authentication, rate limiting, and request routing. API versioning enables service evolution while maintaining client compatibility.

Caching strategies improve microservices performance. Memcached.jl or Redis.jl enable distributed caching. Cache invalidation patterns maintain data consistency. Local caches reduce network traffic. Cache aside and write through patterns support different use cases.

Error handling in distributed systems requires careful consideration. Standardized error responses ensure consistent client handling. Error propagation patterns preserve context across service boundaries. Retry mechanisms handle transient failures. Dead letter queues capture unprocessable messages.

Documentation becomes particularly important in microservices architectures. OpenAPI specifications define service interfaces. Architecture diagrams explain service relationships. Runbooks guide operational procedures. API documentation ensures effective service utilization.

Version management affects multiple aspects of microservices. API versions enable interface evolution. Database schema versions manage data structure changes. Service versions track implementation changes. Documentation versions maintain accuracy.

Performance optimization considers both individual services and system interactions. Profiling identifies bottlenecks within services. Network analysis reveals communication inefficiencies. Resource utilization monitoring enables capacity planning. Caching and buffering improve response times.

Security requires a defense in depth approach. Network segmentation limits attack surfaces. Transport layer security protects communication. Authentication and authorization control access. Security scanning identifies vulnerabilities. Regular updates address security issues.

Building effective microservices with Julia requires understanding both architectural patterns and Julia specific implementation approaches. The language's performance characteristics and rich ecosystem enable efficient implementation of distributed systems while maintaining code clarity and maintainability. Regular review and refinement ensure the architecture continues meeting evolving requirements effectively.

Chapter 42: Real-time Data Processing

Real time data processing represents a critical component in modern data science applications, where systems must handle, analyze, and react to data streams as they arrive. Julia's high performance characteristics make it particularly well suited for processing data in real time, offering both the speed necessary for immediate data handling and the flexibility required for complex analytics.

Stream processing in Julia often begins with data ingestion from various sources. Kafka.jl provides robust integration with Apache Kafka, enabling reliable consumption of high volume data streams. The package supports both batch and record level processing, allowing developers to balance throughput and latency requirements. Consumer groups enable parallel processing of partitioned streams, while offset management ensures reliable message delivery.

WebSockets.jl enables real time data reception over websocket connections, particularly useful for browser based applications or IoT devices. The package provides both client and server implementations, supporting bidirectional communication. Binary message formats like Protocol Buffers or MessagePack, supported through ProtoBuf.jl and MsgPack.jl respectively, offer efficient data serialization for high throughput scenarios.

Window based processing represents a fundamental pattern in stream analytics. Julia's array operations naturally support sliding window calculations. Rolling statistics, moving averages, and other time based aggregations can be implemented efficiently using Julia's built in array operations. OnlineStats.jl specifically targets online learning and streaming statistics, providing algorithms that update incrementally as new data arrives.

Stream joins present unique challenges in real time processing. Window based joins match records from different streams based on temporal proximity. State management becomes crucial, with careful consideration needed for window sizes and state cleanup. Julia's multiple dispatch system enables clean implementation of different join strategies while maintaining high performance.

Pattern detection in real time streams often employs complex event processing techniques. Regular expressions, implemented through Julia's built in regex support, can detect simple patterns. More complex temporal patterns might involve state machines or rule engines. Probabilistic algorithms like Bloom filters, implemented through BloomFilters.jl, enable approximate membership testing with constant memory usage.

Anomaly detection represents another common real time processing requirement. Statistics.jl provides implementations of various statistical tests useful for detecting outliers. Online learning algorithms can adapt to changing data distributions. Julia's multiple dispatch system enables easy implementation of different detection strategies for different data types or scenarios.

State management in stream processing requires careful consideration. In memory state provides fastest access but limited capacity. Redis.jl enables distributed state management when required. State cleanup policies prevent unbounded growth. Checkpointing mechanisms ensure state can be recovered after failures.

Back pressure handling becomes crucial in high volume stream processing. Flow control mechanisms prevent overwhelming downstream components. Buffer management balances throughput and latency. Reactive programming patterns, supported through Observables.jl, enable natural expression of stream processing logic with built in back pressure support.

Performance optimization for real time processing often focuses on minimizing latency. Type stability ensures efficient code execution. Preallocation prevents garbage collection pauses. Thread pool management, through Julia's built in threading support, enables parallel processing while maintaining predictable latency.

Memory management requires special attention in long running stream processors. Regular garbage collection can cause latency spikes. Object pooling reduces allocation overhead. Memory mapped files, supported through Mmap.jl, enable processing of datasets larger than available RAM without explicit management.

Error handling in stream processing must balance reliability and throughput. Dead letter queues capture unprocessable messages for later analysis. Retry policies handle transient failures. Circuit breakers prevent cascade failures when downstream services experience issues. Logging ensures visibility into error conditions without impacting performance.

Monitoring becomes particularly important for real time systems. Metrics collection tracks processing rates, latencies, and error counts. Health checks verify system operation. Alerting ensures timely response to issues. Distributed tracing helps understand message flow through complex systems.

Testing real time systems presents unique challenges. Test data generators simulate various stream conditions. Timing sensitive tests verify latency requirements. Chaos testing ensures robust error handling. Performance testing validates throughput capabilities under realistic conditions.

Deployment considerations for real time processing often involve container orchestration. Kubernetes enables scalable deployment with automatic failover. Resource limits prevent individual processors from overwhelming shared resources. Rolling updates enable deployment without data loss.

Integration with existing systems often requires careful design. Change data capture enables real time processing of database changes. Message transformation handles different data formats. Protocol adaptation enables communication with various external systems. Idempotency ensures reliable processing.

Scaling strategies depend on processing requirements. Horizontal scaling adds processing instances for increased throughput. Vertical scaling increases resources for individual processors. Partitioning enables parallel processing while maintaining order guarantees when required.

Security considerations include both data protection and system access control. Encryption protects sensitive data in transit. Authentication controls system access. Audit logging tracks data access and system changes. Network segregation limits attack surfaces.

Real time processing with Julia enables high performance stream analytics while maintaining code clarity and maintainability. The language's performance characteristics and rich ecosystem support various processing patterns and integration requirements. Regular monitoring and optimization ensure continued effectiveness as requirements evolve.

Chapter 43: ETL Pipeline Development

ETL (Extract, Transform, Load) pipeline development in Julia combines the language's high performance capabilities with robust data processing features to create efficient and scalable data workflows. These pipelines form the backbone of many data science applications, enabling systematic data collection, transformation, and storage for downstream analysis.

The extraction phase typically involves gathering data from various sources. Julia's rich ecosystem provides multiple packages for data access. CSV.jl offers high performance reading of comma separated files, while XLSX.jl handles Excel spreadsheets. For database connections, LibPQ.jl enables PostgreSQL access, MySQL.jl supports MySQL databases, and SQLite.jl provides embedded database functionality. HTTP.jl facilitates API calls for web based data sources.

Connection management represents a crucial aspect of extraction. Connection pooling prevents resource exhaustion when accessing databases. Retry logic handles transient connection failures. Rate limiting ensures compliance with API quotas. Authentication management securely stores and applies credentials while avoiding exposure in source code.

Parallel extraction often improves performance for large datasets. Julia's built in threading and distributed computing capabilities enable concurrent data retrieval. Partitioning strategies divide work across multiple processors. Progress tracking provides visibility into extraction status. Checkpointing enables recovery from failures without restarting entire extractions.

The transformation phase typically involves cleaning, normalizing, and enriching data. DataFrames.jl provides the foundation for many transformation operations. Column type conversion ensures appropriate data representations. Missing value handling fills gaps or removes incomplete records. Deduplication eliminates redundant entries. String normalization standardizes text representations.

Data validation forms an essential part of transformation. Schema validation ensures data meets expected formats. Range checks identify outliers. Referential integrity verification maintains relationships between datasets. Custom validation rules implement business specific requirements. Validation results feed into data quality metrics.

Data enrichment often involves combining multiple sources. Join operations merge related datasets. Lookup tables provide additional attributes. Geographic coding adds location information. Entity resolution matches records referring to the same real world objects. Careful memory management enables processing of datasets larger than available RAM.

Time series specific transformations handle temporal data. DateTime parsing standardizes timestamp formats. Time zone conversion ensures consistent temporal representation. Resampling adjusts data frequency. Gap filling handles missing time points. Season decomposition extracts temporal patterns.

Categorical data often requires special handling during transformation. Level encoding converts categories to numeric representations. Hierarchical categories maintain parent child relationships. Dynamic category management handles previously unseen values. Memory efficient string pooling reduces storage requirements for repeated categories.

The loading phase moves transformed data to its final destination. Bulk loading optimizes insertion performance for large datasets. Transaction management ensures data consistency. Upsert operations handle incremental updates. Partitioning strategies organize data for efficient query access.

Index management optimizes query performance in the target system. Automatic index creation reflects expected query patterns. Index maintenance handles updates. Index optimization balances query performance against storage requirements. Partitioning schemes enable parallel query processing.

Pipeline orchestration coordinates the entire ETL process. Dependency management ensures correct execution order. Resource management prevents system overload. Error handling captures and handles failures. Retry logic handles transient issues. Notification systems alert operators to problems requiring attention.

Monitoring and logging provide visibility into pipeline operation. Performance metrics track processing times and resource usage. Data quality metrics measure transformation effectiveness. Progress tracking enables estimation of completion times. Audit logging maintains records of data modifications.

Incremental processing often improves efficiency for regularly updated data. Change detection identifies modified records. Delta loading updates only changed data. State management tracks processing progress. Cleanup procedures remove unnecessary temporary data.

Version control for transformation logic ensures reproducibility. Code management tracks changes to transformation rules. Configuration management handles environment specific settings. Documentation captures transformation logic and business rules. Testing validates transformation correctness.

Performance optimization focuses on processing efficiency. Type stability ensures efficient code execution. Memory preallocation reduces garbage collection overhead. Parallel processing utilizes available computing resources. Profiling identifies performance bottlenecks.

Error recovery capabilities ensure pipeline reliability. Checkpoint restart enables recovery from failures. Transaction rollback maintains data consistency. State cleanup prevents resource leaks. Error reporting provides detailed failure information for debugging.

Integration with existing systems often requires careful design. Format conversion handles different data representations. Protocol adaptation enables communication with various systems. Authentication management provides secure access. Rate limiting prevents overwhelming target systems.

Security considerations protect sensitive data throughout the pipeline. Encryption secures data in transit and at rest. Access control limits system access. Data masking protects sensitive information. Audit logging tracks data access and modifications.

Testing ensures pipeline reliability. Unit tests verify transformation logic. Integration tests validate end to end operation. Performance tests confirm processing efficiency. Data quality tests verify transformation effectiveness.

Deployment considerations affect pipeline operation. Container deployment enables consistent execution environments. Resource limits prevent system overload. Scaling strategies handle varying data volumes. Monitoring ensures continued effective operation.

ETL pipeline development in Julia combines the language's performance capabilities with robust data processing features to create efficient and maintainable data workflows. The rich ecosystem provides tools for various data sources and transformations, while built in features enable parallel processing and error handling. Regular monitoring and optimization ensure continued effectiveness as requirements evolve.

Chapter 44: Scheduling and Job Management

Scheduling and job management represent critical components of production data science systems, ensuring reliable execution of computational tasks while optimizing resource utilization. Julia provides several approaches and packages for implementing robust job scheduling systems that can handle both periodic tasks and complex computational workflows.

The Scheduler.jl package offers a foundation for scheduling tasks in Julia applications. It provides functionality for defining jobs, setting execution schedules, and managing job dependencies. Tasks can be scheduled using cron-style expressions, allowing precise control over execution timing. The package supports both one-time and recurring job execution, making it suitable for various scheduling needs from periodic data updates to regular model retraining.

Job definitions typically include several key components. The task function contains the actual work to be performed. Schedule specifications determine when the job should run. Resource requirements define computational needs like memory and CPU cores. Priority settings influence execution order when multiple jobs compete for resources. Timeout values prevent jobs from running indefinitely.

Dependency management ensures jobs execute in the correct order. Direct dependencies specify explicit ordering requirements. Resource dependencies prevent concurrent execution of jobs competing for the same resources. Time based dependencies coordinate jobs that must run in specific sequences. The scheduler handles dependency resolution and ensures proper execution order.

Error handling forms a crucial part of job management. Retry policies specify how to handle failed jobs. Backoff strategies prevent system overload from repeated retries. Failure notifications alert operators to problems requiring attention. Job logs capture execution details for debugging. State management tracks job status throughout execution.

Resource management prevents system overload from concurrent job execution. Resource pools track available computational resources. Allocation strategies distribute resources across jobs. Preemption policies handle resource contention. Usage monitoring ensures efficient resource utilization. Cleanup procedures release resources after job completion.

Distributed job execution often improves performance for computational workloads. The Distributed.jl package enables job distribution across multiple processors or machines. Work stealing balances load across workers. Fault tolerance handles worker failures. Result collection aggregates distributed computation results. Network failure handling ensures reliable distributed execution.

Queue management organizes pending jobs. Priority queues ensure important jobs run first. Fair scheduling prevents job starvation. Queue monitoring tracks backlog size. Queue cleanup removes completed or expired jobs. Rate limiting prevents queue overflow.

State persistence ensures system reliability across restarts. Job state storage preserves execution status. Schedule persistence maintains timing information. Result storage retains job outputs. Configuration persistence preserves system settings. Recovery procedures restore state after system restart.

Monitoring provides visibility into job execution. Status dashboards show current system state. Performance metrics track execution times and resource usage. Queue metrics monitor workflow health. Alert systems notify operators of problems. Historical metrics enable trend analysis.

Integration with external systems often requires careful coordination. API endpoints enable external job submission. Status reporting provides execution visibility. Result delivery returns job outputs. Authentication ensures secure access. Rate limiting prevents system overload.

Configuration management handles system settings. Environment specific configuration adapts to different deployments. Secret management securely stores sensitive information. Dynamic configuration enables runtime adjustments. Version control tracks configuration changes.

Testing ensures reliable job execution. Unit tests verify individual job functions. Integration tests validate scheduling behavior. Load tests confirm system capacity. Failure testing verifies error handling. Recovery testing validates system restoration.

Performance optimization focuses on execution efficiency. Job batching reduces overhead for small tasks. Resource pooling minimizes allocation overhead. Caching prevents redundant computation. Profiling identifies performance bottlenecks. Optimization adjusts system parameters for better performance.

Security considerations protect system operation. Access control limits system usage. Audit logging tracks job submission and execution. Resource isolation prevents interference between jobs. Credential management handles secure authentication.

Scaling capabilities handle varying workloads. Horizontal scaling adds processing capacity. Auto scaling adjusts resources to demand. Load balancing distributes work across resources. Capacity planning ensures sufficient resources.

Maintenance procedures ensure continued system health. Log rotation prevents disk space exhaustion. State cleanup removes unnecessary data. Index optimization maintains database performance. Configuration updates adapt to changing requirements.

Documentation captures system operation details. Architecture documentation describes system design. Operation procedures guide system management. Troubleshooting guides assist problem resolution. API documentation enables system integration.

Development workflows support system evolution. Version control tracks code changes. Testing validates modifications. Deployment procedures update production systems. Rollback capabilities handle failed updates.

Production deployment requires careful preparation. Environment setup ensures required resources. Configuration verification confirms system settings. Initial state preparation establishes starting conditions. Monitoring confirmation verifies system visibility.

Job scheduling and management in Julia combines the language's performance capabilities with robust execution control to create reliable computational workflows. The available tools and packages enable development of sophisticated scheduling systems that can handle complex dependencies while ensuring efficient resource utilization. Regular monitoring and maintenance ensure continued effective operation as requirements evolve.

Chapter 45: Resource Management

Resource management in production data science systems requires careful consideration to ensure optimal utilization of computational resources while maintaining system stability and performance. Julia provides several tools and approaches for implementing effective resource management strategies in data science applications.

Memory management forms a fundamental aspect of resource control. Julia's garbage collector automatically handles memory deallocation, but understanding its behavior helps optimize resource usage. The GC.gc() function enables manual garbage collection when needed. Memory pools can be implemented to reuse allocated memory for frequently created and destroyed objects, reducing allocation overhead. Monitoring memory usage through @allocated and @time macros helps identify memory intensive operations.

CPU resource management ensures efficient processor utilization. Thread pools manage concurrent execution of computational tasks. The Base.Threads module provides primitives for thread management, while ThreadPools.jl offers higher level abstractions. Processor affinity settings can bind computations to specific cores. Load balancing algorithms distribute work evenly across available processors. Priority based scheduling ensures critical tasks receive necessary compute resources.

Storage resource management handles disk space utilization. File system monitoring tracks available space. Cleanup policies remove unnecessary temporary files. Data archival moves infrequently accessed data to cheaper storage. Compression reduces storage requirements. File handle limits prevent resource exhaustion from too many open files. Buffer management optimizes I/O performance.

Network resource management controls bandwidth utilization. Quality of service policies prioritize critical traffic. Rate limiting prevents network saturation. Connection pooling reduces overhead for frequent connections. Timeout settings prevent hung connections from consuming resources. Retry policies handle transient network failures.

Database resource management ensures efficient database utilization. Connection pools maintain ready database connections. Query optimization reduces resource requirements. Index management improves query performance. Transaction management prevents resource locks. Partitioning distributes data across storage resources.

GPU resource management optimizes accelerator utilization. Memory transfer scheduling minimizes data movement overhead. Kernel scheduling maximizes GPU utilization. Multi GPU management coordinates across devices. Memory management handles limited GPU memory. Error handling addresses device failures.

Container resource management controls containerized application resources. Resource limits prevent container overflow. Resource guarantees ensure minimum available resources. Resource monitoring tracks utilization. Scaling policies adjust resource allocation. Cleanup procedures release container resources.

Cloud resource management optimizes cloud service utilization. Auto scaling adjusts resource allocation to demand. Cost optimization balances resource usage and expenses. Resource tagging tracks resource ownership. Lifecycle policies manage resource creation and deletion. Multi region management coordinates across locations.

Distributed resource management coordinates across multiple systems. Resource discovery identifies available resources. Resource allocation distributes work across systems. Resource recovery handles system failures. State management maintains resource status. Synchronization coordinates resource usage.

Cache resource management optimizes cache utilization. Cache sizing balances memory usage and hit rates. Eviction policies manage limited cache space. Warm up procedures prepare caches for use. Monitoring tracks cache effectiveness. Cleanup removes stale cache entries.

Queue resource management handles message queue systems. Queue sizing prevents memory exhaustion. Consumer scaling adjusts processing capacity. Dead letter handling manages failed messages. Monitoring tracks queue depths. Cleanup removes processed messages.

Temporary resource management handles intermediate computation results. Storage allocation provides working space. Cleanup removes unnecessary temporaries. Size limits prevent resource exhaustion. Monitoring tracks temporary resource usage. Recovery handles cleanup failures.

Resource monitoring provides visibility into resource utilization. Metrics collection tracks resource usage. Alerting notifies of resource issues. Trending analyzes usage patterns. Capacity planning projects future needs. Documentation records resource requirements.

Resource optimization improves utilization efficiency. Profiling identifies resource bottlenecks. Tuning adjusts resource parameters. Benchmarking measures improvement. Testing validates optimization changes. Documentation captures optimization decisions.

Security aspects of resource management protect system resources. Access control limits resource usage. Audit logging tracks resource utilization. Resource isolation prevents interference. Credential management controls resource access. Encryption protects sensitive resources.

Configuration management handles resource settings. Environment configuration adapts to deployments. Secret management secures sensitive settings. Dynamic configuration enables runtime adjustment. Version control tracks configuration changes.

Testing validates resource management behavior. Unit tests verify management functions. Integration tests validate resource coordination. Load tests confirm capacity limits. Failure testing verifies error handling. Recovery testing validates restoration procedures.

Documentation captures resource management details. Architecture documentation describes resource design. Operation procedures guide resource management. Troubleshooting guides assist problem resolution. API documentation enables integration.

Development workflows support resource management evolution. Version control tracks implementation changes. Testing validates modifications. Deployment procedures update production systems. Rollback capabilities handle failed updates.

Production deployment requires careful resource preparation. Environment setup ensures required resources. Configuration verification confirms settings. Initial state preparation establishes starting conditions. Monitoring confirmation verifies visibility.

Effective resource management combines Julia's capabilities with careful planning and implementation to ensure optimal resource utilization while maintaining system stability and performance. Regular monitoring and maintenance ensure continued effective operation as requirements evolve.

Chapter 46: Security Best Practices

Security best practices are essential for protecting data science applications and ensuring the confidentiality, integrity, and availability of sensitive data and computational resources. When developing production data science systems in Julia, several key security considerations must be addressed.

Authentication and authorization form the foundation of security controls. Julia applications should implement robust user authentication using industry standard mechanisms like JSON Web Tokens (JWT) or OAuth2. The JWT.jl package provides tools for working with JWTs, while OAuth2.jl enables OAuth2 integration. Role based access control (RBAC) ensures users can only access authorized resources. Permission management tracks and enforces access rights.

Data encryption protects sensitive information. Julia's built in cryptography functions enable encryption of data at rest and in transit. The OpenSSL.jl package provides additional cryptographic capabilities. Transport Layer Security (TLS) secures network communications. Key management handles encryption key lifecycle. Certificate management maintains TLS certificates.

Secure coding practices prevent common vulnerabilities. Input validation prevents injection attacks. Output encoding prevents cross site scripting. Error handling avoids information disclosure. Memory management prevents buffer overflows. Type safety reduces exploitation opportunities. The Security.jl package provides security focused utilities.

Dependency management ensures secure third party code. Package version pinning prevents unexpected changes. Dependency scanning identifies known vulnerabilities. Vendor assessment evaluates package security. License compliance confirms usage rights. Alternative package evaluation provides options.

Configuration security protects sensitive settings. Environment variables secure credentials. Secret management systems protect sensitive data. Configuration encryption prevents exposure. Access control limits configuration visibility. Audit logging tracks configuration changes.

Network security controls protect system communications. Firewall rules limit network access. Network segmentation isolates components. Intrusion detection monitors for attacks. DDoS protection prevents resource exhaustion. VPN access secures remote connectivity.

Container security hardens containerized applications. Image scanning identifies vulnerabilities. Resource limits prevent container breakout. Network policies control container communication. Secret injection secures credentials. Runtime protection monitors container behavior.

Cloud security leverages provider capabilities. Identity management controls access. Resource encryption protects data. Network security groups limit connectivity. Logging enables audit trails. Compliance tools ensure policy adherence.

Database security protects stored data. Access control limits data visibility. Query parameterization prevents SQL injection. Encryption secures sensitive data. Audit logging tracks access. Backup encryption protects copies.

API security controls external interfaces. Authentication verifies clients. Rate limiting prevents abuse. Input validation sanitizes requests. Output filtering prevents data leakage. CORS policies control access.

Monitoring enables security visibility. Log aggregation centralizes security data. Alert rules identify threats. SIEM integration enables analysis. Incident response handles issues. Retention policies maintain history.

Security testing validates controls. Penetration testing identifies vulnerabilities. Security scanning checks known issues. Compliance testing verifies requirements. Red team exercises test defenses. Bug bounty programs incentivize disclosure.

Incident response handles security events. Response procedures guide actions. Investigation tools support analysis. Communication plans notify stakeholders. Recovery procedures restore systems. Post mortems capture lessons.

Security documentation records controls. Architecture documents describe security design. Policies define requirements. Procedures guide implementation. Standards specify baselines. Guidelines provide recommendations.

Compliance management ensures regulatory adherence. Requirements tracking maps controls. Evidence collection documents compliance. Audit support enables verification. Gap analysis identifies needs. Remediation planning addresses gaps.

Security training develops team capabilities. Awareness training builds knowledge. Technical training develops skills. Policy training ensures understanding. Exercise participation practices response. Certification validates expertise.

Change management maintains security. Impact analysis evaluates changes. Testing validates modifications. Approval processes control changes. Implementation procedures guide updates. Rollback capabilities handle issues.

Vulnerability management addresses weaknesses. Scanning identifies issues. Risk assessment evaluates impact. Prioritization guides remediation. Patch management fixes vulnerabilities. Verification confirms fixes.

Access management controls system usage. User provisioning grants access. Access review validates rights. Access revocation removes privileges. Password management ensures security. Multi factor authentication strengthens controls.

Data classification guides protection. Classification schemes categorize data. Handling requirements specify controls. Labeling identifies sensitivity. Access policies enforce requirements. Disposal ensures secure removal.

Audit capability enables verification. Logging captures activity. Log protection prevents tampering. Analysis tools examine logs. Reporting provides visibility. Retention maintains history.

Development security integrates controls. Secure development lifecycle guides process. Code review identifies issues. Security testing validates controls. Security tools support development. Documentation captures decisions.

Production deployment requires security preparation. Environment hardening applies controls. Configuration validation verifies settings. Security testing confirms controls. Monitoring verification ensures visibility.

Regular security assessment maintains effectiveness. Control testing validates operation. Vulnerability assessment identifies weaknesses. Configuration review verifies settings. Policy compliance confirms adherence. Risk assessment evaluates posture.

Implementing comprehensive security controls protects Julia data science applications while enabling authorized access and usage. Regular review and updates ensure controls remain effective as threats evolve and requirements change.

Chapter 47: Integration with Python Libraries

While Julia provides exceptional performance and native capabilities, many data scientists need to leverage existing Python libraries in their workflows. This chapter explores how to seamlessly integrate Python libraries into Julia applications while maintaining performance and reliability in production environments.

The PyCall.jl package serves as the primary bridge between Julia and Python, allowing Julia code to directly call Python modules and functions. Setting up PyCall requires a working Python installation, which can be managed through Julia's built in conda environment or by pointing to an existing Python installation. The package automatically handles type conversions between Julia and Python, making the integration nearly transparent to end users.

A key consideration when using PyCall is managing Python dependencies. The Conda.jl package provides tools for creating and managing isolated conda environments directly from Julia. This enables reproducible deployment by explicitly specifying required Python packages and versions. In production settings, it's recommended to create a dedicated conda environment for each application to prevent dependency conflicts.

Converting data between Julia and Python formats requires understanding type mappings. Numeric types generally convert automatically, with Julia's Int64 mapping to Python's int and Float64 to float. Arrays convert between Julia arrays and NumPy arrays, preserving dimensionality and element types. Strings, dictionaries, and other basic types also have natural mappings. However, custom types may require explicit conversion logic.

DataFrames present special considerations for interoperability. The pandas.jl package provides direct conversion between Julia DataFrames and pandas DataFrames. While conversion is straightforward, frequent conversions can impact performance. When working with large datasets, it's often better to perform operations in a single language before converting results. The Tables.jl interface enables generic conversions between tabular data formats.

Scientific computing libraries like NumPy, SciPy, and scikit learn are commonly used through PyCall. While Julia provides native alternatives, legacy code or specific algorithm implementations may necessitate using Python libraries. The PyCall interface allows calling these libraries with minimal overhead. However, frequent crossing between Julia and Python can impact performance, so operations should be batched when possible.

Machine learning workflows often require Python libraries like TensorFlow or PyTorch. While Flux.jl provides native deep learning capabilities, pretrained models or specialized architectures may require Python integration. The PyCall interface enables loading and running models, with tensors converting between frameworks. Production deployments should consider serializing models to optimize performance.

Visualization libraries like matplotlib and seaborn can complement Julia's plotting capabilities. PyPlot.jl provides a Julia interface to matplotlib, while direct PyCall usage enables access to other visualization libraries. When generating visualizations in production, consider caching results and limiting interactive features to improve performance.

Natural language processing often leverages Python libraries like NLTK or spaCy. While Julia has growing NLP capabilities, accessing existing models and pipelines may require Python integration. The PyCall interface enables using these libraries while performing compute intensive operations in Julia. Text data generally converts smoothly between languages.

Image processing frequently uses Python libraries like OpenCV or PIL. While Julia provides Images.jl, specific algorithms or existing pipelines may require Python integration. The PyCall interface handles image data conversion, though large batch operations should minimize conversions to maintain performance.

Web frameworks and API clients often have mature Python implementations. While Julia provides HTTP.jl and other web tools, integrating existing Python clients can speed development. The PyCall interface enables using these libraries while handling computation in Julia. Connection pooling and request batching can optimize performance.

Production deployment requires careful management of Python dependencies. Docker containers should include both Julia and Python environments with explicit version pinning. Environment variables configure Python paths and settings. Monitoring should track both Julia and Python resource usage. Error handling must account for both languages.

Testing integrated applications requires validating both Julia and Python components. Unit tests should verify type conversions and error handling. Integration tests confirm end to end functionality. Performance tests measure conversion overhead. Continuous integration should test both languages.

Error handling becomes more complex with language integration. Python exceptions must be caught and converted to Julia exceptions. Stack traces should preserve context from both languages. Logging should capture details from both environments. Recovery procedures must handle both languages.

Monitoring integrated applications requires tracking both Julia and Python metrics. Resource usage monitoring watches both runtimes. Performance monitoring measures conversion overhead. Error monitoring catches issues in both languages. Logging aggregates information from both environments.

Security considerations span both languages. Dependency scanning must check both Julia and Python packages. Input validation happens in both contexts. Network security applies to both runtimes. Access controls cover both environments.

Documentation should clearly specify Python dependencies and version requirements. Installation instructions must cover both languages. API documentation should indicate language boundaries. Troubleshooting guides should address both environments.

Performance optimization requires understanding integration overhead. Profiling identifies costly conversions. Batching reduces boundary crossings. Caching prevents redundant operations. Native implementations may improve performance.

While Python integration enables leveraging existing libraries, production applications should carefully consider the tradeoffs. Converting frequently between languages impacts performance. Maintaining dependencies in two languages increases complexity. Native Julia implementations may provide better long term maintainability.

The Julia ecosystem continues growing, potentially reducing the need for Python integration over time. However, the ability to leverage Python libraries remains valuable for practical development. Understanding how to effectively integrate Python while maintaining production quality enables building robust applications that leverage the strengths of both languages.

Chapter 48: Integration with R Packages

Chapter 48 focuses on integrating R packages with Julia, providing data scientists a bridge to leverage R's extensive statistical and analytical capabilities while maintaining Julia's performance advantages.

The RCall.jl package serves as the primary interface between Julia and R, enabling seamless interaction with R's extensive package ecosystem. Similar to Python integration, RCall allows Julia programs to directly execute R code and access R functions while handling type conversions automatically. Setting up RCall requires a working R installation, which can be managed independently or through Julia's package manager.

Managing R dependencies requires careful consideration in production environments. While R packages can be installed through RCall, it's recommended to maintain a separate R environment for each application to ensure reproducibility. Tools like renv in R can help manage package versions, while Docker containers can encapsulate both Julia and R environments for deployment.

Data type conversion between Julia and R follows natural mappings. Numeric vectors in R convert to Julia arrays, with preservation of missing values through Julia's missing type. R data frames convert to Julia DataFrames, maintaining column names and types. Factor variables in R map to categorical arrays in Julia. The conversion system handles most common types automatically, though complex objects may require custom conversion logic.

Statistical analysis often leverages R's mature packages like stats, lme4, or survival. While Julia provides growing statistical capabilities, specific implementations or established methodologies may necessitate R integration. RCall enables using these packages efficiently, though operations should be batched to minimize conversion overhead. The

StatisticalRethinking.jl package demonstrates effective R integration for Bayesian analysis.

Visualization libraries like ggplot2 offer sophisticated plotting capabilities that complement Julia's options. RCall enables direct use of ggplot2, while packages like RDatasets.jl facilitate access to R's built in datasets. When generating plots in production, consider caching results and managing memory usage, as R's plotting system can be resource intensive.

Bioinformatics workflows often require R's Bioconductor packages. While Julia has BioJulia, accessing established R pipelines may be necessary. RCall enables using these packages while performing computationally intensive operations in Julia. Sequence data and genomic annotations convert effectively between languages, though large datasets require careful memory management.

Time series analysis frequently uses R packages like forecast or xts. While Julia provides TimeSeries.jl, specific forecasting methods or existing analyses may require R integration. RCall handles time series data conversion, maintaining timestamps and frequencies. Production systems should optimize for bulk operations to reduce conversion overhead.

Spatial analysis often leverages R's sp or sf packages. While Julia provides GeoInterface.jl, accessing existing spatial analysis tools may require R integration. RCall handles conversion of spatial data structures, though large geometric operations should minimize language transitions for performance.

Text mining and natural language processing may use R packages like tm or quanteda. While Julia's text processing capabilities are growing, accessing established R workflows can be valuable. RCall enables using these packages while performing parallel processing in Julia. Document term matrices and corpus objects require careful memory management.

Production deployment with R integration requires additional considerations. Docker containers must include both Julia and R environments with specific package versions. Environment variables configure R paths and settings. Resource monitoring should track both Julia and R processes. Error handling must account for both language contexts.

Testing integrated applications becomes more complex with dual language components. Unit tests should verify data conversions and error handling. Integration tests confirm end to end functionality. Performance tests measure conversion overhead. Continuous integration pipelines must test both Julia and R components.

Error handling requires managing exceptions from both languages. R errors must be caught and converted to Julia exceptions. Stack traces should maintain context across language boundaries. Logging systems must capture information from both environments. Recovery procedures need to handle both language contexts.

Documentation becomes particularly important with R integration. Package dependencies and version requirements must be clearly specified for both languages. Installation instructions should cover both environments. API documentation should indicate language transitions. Troubleshooting guides need to address both contexts.

Performance optimization requires careful attention to language boundaries. Profiling helps identify costly conversions. Batching operations reduces transition overhead. Caching prevents redundant computations. Native Julia implementations may provide better performance for critical components.

Memory management requires special consideration when working with two language runtimes. Large datasets should minimize copies between languages. Garbage collection behavior may need tuning for both environments. Resource limits should account for both language processes.

Security considerations span both language environments. Dependency scanning must cover both Julia and R packages. Input validation happens in both contexts. Network security applies to both runtimes. Access controls must cover both environments.

While R integration enables leveraging its statistical ecosystem, production applications should carefully evaluate the tradeoffs. Converting data between languages impacts performance. Maintaining dependencies in two languages increases complexity. Native Julia implementations may provide better long term maintainability.

The Julia ecosystem continues expanding its statistical capabilities, potentially reducing the need for R integration over time. However, the ability to leverage R's extensive package ecosystem remains valuable for many analytical workflows. Understanding how to effectively integrate R while maintaining production quality enables building robust applications that combine the statistical depth of R with Julia's performance advantages.

Chapter 49: Web Scraping and APIs

Web scraping and APIs represent essential tools in modern data science, enabling automated data collection from websites and integration with various web services. Julia provides robust capabilities for both web scraping and API interaction through several powerful packages.

HTTP.jl serves as the foundation for web interactions in Julia, offering a comprehensive set of tools for making HTTP requests. The package supports all standard HTTP methods, custom headers, authentication, and automatic handling of redirects. For production applications, HTTP.jl provides connection pooling, timeout configuration, and retry mechanisms essential for reliable data collection.

When working with REST APIs, JSON3.jl provides high performance JSON parsing and serialization. Unlike Python's requests library, Julia's approach separates HTTP handling from data parsing, allowing for more flexible and efficient processing. The package automatically handles Julia type conversion, though custom structs may require specific serialization methods. Production applications should implement proper error handling for malformed responses and rate limiting.

Web scraping in Julia typically employs Gumbo.jl for HTML parsing and Cascadia.jl for CSS selector based element extraction. These packages work together to provide functionality similar to Python's Beautiful Soup. Gumbo.jl creates a DOM tree representation of HTML documents, while Cascadia.jl enables precise targeting of elements using familiar CSS syntax. Production scraping applications should implement polite crawling practices, including respecting robots.txt and implementing appropriate delays between requests.

Authentication handling varies by API type. OAuth implementations can leverage OAuth.jl, while basic authentication is handled directly through HTTP.jl. API keys and credentials should be managed securely, preferably through environment variables or secure credential storage systems. Production applications must implement proper token refresh mechanisms and handle authentication failures gracefully.

Rate limiting represents a critical consideration for both web scraping and API interactions. Julia's concurrent programming features enable implementing sophisticated rate limiting strategies. Tokenizing approaches can manage multiple API keys, while adaptive rate limiting can respond to server responses. Production systems should implement backoff strategies for failed requests and maintain usage metrics to prevent quota exhaustion.

Data extraction from HTML requires careful handling of text normalization, character encoding, and structural variations. Regular expressions in Julia, while similar to Python's re module, offer additional performance optimizations. Unicode handling through Julia's native UTF-8 support ensures proper processing of international content. Production applications should implement robust parsing logic to handle malformed HTML and inconsistent formatting.

API response handling must account for various data formats beyond JSON. XML.jl provides XML parsing capabilities, while YAML.jl handles YAML formats. Binary data can be processed efficiently using Julia's array operations. Production systems should implement proper content type checking and format specific error handling. Large responses may require streaming processing to manage memory efficiently.

Concurrent scraping and API requests leverage Julia's native parallel processing capabilities. The AsyncHTTP.jl package enables asynchronous HTTP requests, while distributed computing features allow scaling across multiple machines. Production systems should implement proper error handling for network failures and timeouts, with automatic retry mechanisms for transient failures.

Session management becomes important for websites requiring login or maintaining state. HTTP.jl's cookie handling capabilities enable maintaining sessions across requests. Production applications should implement proper session refresh mechanisms and handle session expiration gracefully. Security considerations include protecting session tokens and implementing proper logout procedures.

Proxy support may be necessary for accessing certain websites or distributing requests. HTTP.jl provides built in proxy configuration options, while rotating proxy implementations can help avoid IP based rate limiting. Production systems should implement proper proxy health checking and fallback mechanisms.

Data storage considerations include choosing appropriate formats and implementing efficient write patterns. CSV.jl and Arrow.jl provide high performance options for structured data, while binary formats may be more appropriate for raw responses. Production systems should implement proper file handling with atomic writes and appropriate error handling.

Monitoring and logging become critical for production web scraping and API operations. Logging.jl enables detailed request tracking, while custom metrics can track success rates and performance. Production systems should implement alerting for failure conditions and maintain detailed audit trails of all requests.

Schema evolution handling ensures robust parsing as APIs or website structures change. StructTypes.jl provides flexible type mapping capabilities, while version tagged types can handle multiple response formats. Production systems should implement schema validation and maintain compatibility with historical data formats.

Error recovery strategies must account for various failure modes including network issues, rate limiting, and parsing errors. Retry mechanisms should implement exponential backoff, while circuit breakers can prevent cascade failures. Production systems should maintain detailed error logs and implement appropriate fallback behaviors.

Testing web scraping and API interaction requires careful consideration of external dependencies. Recording and replaying HTTP interactions through HTTP.jl's built in testing utilities enables reliable unit testing. Integration tests should use dedicated test endpoints or carefully controlled live resources. Performance testing must account for network variability and rate limiting.

Documentation becomes particularly important for web scraping and API integration. API specifications should be clearly documented, including authentication requirements and rate limits. Scraping logic should document CSS selectors and extraction assumptions. Production runbooks should include troubleshooting guides for common failure modes.

Long term maintenance requires monitoring for API changes and website structure updates. Automated testing can detect breaking changes, while version controlled schemas help manage evolution. Production systems should implement proper alerting for unexpected response patterns and maintain upgrade procedures for API versions.

Web scraping and API integration in Julia combines high performance with robust error handling and scalability features. While the ecosystem may have fewer specialized packages than Python, Julia's core capabilities enable building production quality data collection systems that can scale effectively while maintaining reliability and maintainability.

Chapter 50: Data Versioning

Data versioning represents a critical aspect of production data science workflows, ensuring reproducibility, traceability, and collaboration across teams. Julia's ecosystem provides several approaches to version control and manage data assets effectively throughout their lifecycle.

DataVersions.jl offers a foundational framework for versioning datasets, providing functionality similar to DVC in Python but with native Julia integration. The package implements content addressable storage, allowing efficient handling of large datasets while maintaining version history. Unlike traditional version control systems focused on code, DataVersions.jl optimizes for binary data and large files common in data science workflows.

Hash based tracking enables efficient storage of dataset versions by identifying duplicate content across versions. This approach minimizes storage requirements while maintaining complete version history. Production systems should implement appropriate garbage collection policies to manage storage growth while preserving essential historical versions.

Metadata management becomes crucial for effective data versioning. Julia's type system enables creating rich metadata structures that can track provenance, processing steps, and quality metrics. Production applications should implement consistent metadata schemas and maintain proper documentation of all transformations applied to datasets.

Integration with Git workflows allows coupling data versions with code versions. While Git LFS provides large file support, specialized data versioning tools offer better performance for data science workflows. Production systems should implement proper branching strategies that account for both code and data evolution.

Dataset dependencies require careful tracking to ensure reproducibility. DataVersions.jl provides dependency graph functionality that can track relationships between derived datasets. Production applications should implement proper dependency documentation and maintain compatibility matrices for different dataset versions.

Feature evolution tracking becomes important when dealing with machine learning datasets. Julia's type system enables implementing schema validation and evolution tracking. Production systems should maintain clear documentation of feature definitions and implement proper migration paths for schema changes.

Distributed storage support enables efficient handling of large scale datasets across multiple storage locations. Julia's distributed computing capabilities can be leveraged to implement efficient data transfer and synchronization. Production systems should implement proper access control and maintain consistency across distributed copies.

Versioning for streaming data presents unique challenges. Buffer based approaches can capture temporal snapshots, while change tracking systems can record incremental updates. Production applications should implement appropriate retention policies and maintain proper audit trails of data modifications.

Collaboration features enable multiple team members to work with versioned datasets. Access control mechanisms ensure proper data governance, while merge capabilities handle concurrent modifications. Production systems should implement proper conflict resolution strategies and maintain clear documentation of sharing protocols.

Quality assurance becomes essential when versioning datasets. Automated validation can verify data integrity and schema compliance, while quality metrics can track dataset characteristics over time. Production applications should implement proper testing protocols for dataset versions and maintain quality thresholds.

Integration with data catalogs enables discovery and documentation of dataset versions. Julia packages can interface with external catalog systems or implement custom cataloging solutions. Production systems should maintain proper metadata indexing and implement search capabilities for dataset discovery.

Backup and recovery strategies must account for versioned datasets. Incremental backup approaches can efficiently handle large datasets, while recovery procedures must maintain version integrity. Production applications should implement proper disaster recovery procedures and maintain regular backup verification.

Performance considerations include efficient storage formats and access patterns. Julia's memory mapping capabilities enable working with large datasets efficiently, while compression can reduce storage requirements. Production systems should implement appropriate caching strategies and optimize access patterns for common operations.

Security requirements must be considered when implementing data versioning. Access controls should be granular enough to manage permissions at the version level, while audit trails track usage patterns. Production applications should implement proper encryption for sensitive data and maintain compliance with data protection regulations.

Integration testing becomes important when working with versioned datasets. Test suites should verify version compatibility and validate transformation pipelines. Production systems should implement automated testing for version transitions and maintain proper test coverage across dataset versions.

Documentation plays a crucial role in data versioning. Version histories should include clear descriptions of changes and rationale for modifications. Production applications should maintain proper changelog documentation and implement clear versioning conventions.

Monitoring requirements include tracking storage usage, access patterns, and version evolution. Custom metrics can track dataset characteristics over time, while alerts can identify potential issues. Production systems should implement proper monitoring dashboards and maintain alerting thresholds.

Migration strategies become necessary when upgrading versioning systems or moving between storage platforms. Careful planning ensures version history preservation and maintains data integrity. Production applications should implement proper migration testing and maintain detailed procedures for platform transitions.

Cleanup procedures must balance storage efficiency with version preservation. Retention policies should consider both business requirements and technical constraints. Production systems should implement proper archival procedures and maintain clear documentation of retention decisions.

Data versioning in Julia combines robust technical capabilities with practical considerations for production deployment. While the ecosystem continues to evolve, existing tools enable building sophisticated versioning systems that support modern data science workflows while maintaining reliability and scalability.

Chapter 51: Model Deployment

Model deployment represents a critical phase in the machine learning lifecycle, transforming carefully crafted models into production ready assets that deliver business value. Julia provides several approaches to deploying models effectively, combining performance with maintainability.

Model serialization forms the foundation of deployment workflows. Julia's native serialization capabilities through BSON.jl and JLD2.jl enable efficient model storage and loading. Production systems should implement proper versioning of serialized models and maintain compatibility checks during loading. The choice of serialization format impacts both storage efficiency and loading performance, with binary formats typically offering better performance for large models.

Deployment environments require careful consideration of dependencies. Julia's package manager enables creating reproducible environments through Project.toml and Manifest.toml files. Production systems should maintain proper dependency locking and implement compatibility testing across different environment configurations. Container based deployment using Docker or similar tools provides additional isolation and reproducibility.

Model serving architectures vary based on application requirements. RESTful APIs implemented through HTTP.jl or similar packages enable synchronous inference, while message queue based approaches support asynchronous processing. Production systems should implement proper load balancing and maintain appropriate scaling policies based on traffic patterns. The choice between synchronous and asynchronous serving depends on latency requirements and resource constraints.

Performance optimization becomes crucial during deployment. Julia's compiler optimizations and type system enable efficient model execution. Production systems should implement proper warm up procedures and maintain performance monitoring. Batch processing capabilities can improve throughput for certain workloads, while proper resource allocation ensures consistent performance under load.

Hardware acceleration through GPUs or specialized processors requires specific deployment considerations. CUDA.jl and similar packages enable leveraging accelerated hardware, while proper driver management ensures compatibility. Production systems should implement proper fallback mechanisms and maintain performance metrics across different hardware configurations. Resource allocation strategies should account for specialized hardware requirements.

Model versioning during deployment requires careful management. Version control systems should track both model artifacts and associated metadata. Production systems should implement proper rollback procedures and maintain compatibility matrices across model versions. A/B testing capabilities enable controlled deployment of new versions while maintaining service stability.

Monitoring requirements include tracking both model performance and system health. Custom metrics can capture prediction quality and resource utilization, while logging enables detailed troubleshooting. Production systems should implement proper alerting thresholds and maintain dashboard visibility into key metrics. Performance degradation detection enables proactive maintenance.

Security considerations become paramount during deployment. Access controls should manage both model access and prediction endpoints, while encryption protects sensitive data. Production systems should implement proper authentication mechanisms and maintain compliance with security requirements. Regular security audits ensure ongoing protection of deployed assets.

Scalability requirements influence deployment architecture. Horizontal scaling through multiple instances enables handling increased load, while vertical scaling leverages more powerful hardware. Production systems should implement proper auto scaling policies and maintain performance under varying load conditions. Resource utilization monitoring helps optimize scaling decisions.

Integration testing becomes essential for deployed models. Test suites should verify both functional correctness and performance characteristics. Production systems should implement automated deployment testing and maintain proper test coverage across different scenarios. Integration with CI/CD pipelines enables automated validation during deployment.

Documentation requirements include both technical specifications and operational procedures. Deployment documentation should cover installation, configuration, and troubleshooting. Production systems should maintain proper runbooks and implement clear incident response procedures. Knowledge sharing enables effective operation across different team members.

Error handling requires careful consideration during deployment. Proper exception handling ensures graceful failure modes, while retry mechanisms handle transient issues. Production systems should implement proper fallback strategies and maintain clear error reporting. Circuit breakers can prevent cascade failures in distributed systems.

Resource management becomes important for deployed models. Memory usage patterns should be monitored and optimized, while CPU utilization requires careful balancing. Production systems should implement proper resource limits and maintain monitoring of usage patterns. Garbage collection tuning may be necessary for optimal performance.

Deployment automation enables consistent and reliable updates. Automated deployment scripts handle routine operations, while validation steps ensure proper execution. Production systems should implement proper deployment verification and maintain rollback capabilities. Blue green deployment strategies enable zero downtime updates.

Configuration management requires careful handling during deployment. Environment specific settings should be properly externalized, while sensitive information requires secure storage. Production systems should implement proper configuration validation and maintain clear documentation of available options. Version control of configuration ensures traceability.

Logging strategies become crucial for deployed models. Structured logging enables efficient analysis, while log levels control verbosity. Production systems should implement proper log rotation and maintain archival procedures. Log analysis tools enable identifying patterns and troubleshooting issues.

Health checking capabilities ensure proper operation. Readiness and liveness probes enable automated monitoring, while custom health metrics track application specific status. Production systems should implement proper health check endpoints and maintain appropriate thresholds. Automated recovery procedures can handle common failure modes.

Deployment in Julia combines robust technical capabilities with practical operational considerations. While specific requirements vary across applications, following established patterns and best practices enables building reliable and maintainable deployed systems. Regular review and updates ensure continued effectiveness of deployment strategies as requirements evolve.

Chapter 52: Model Serving

Model serving represents the critical infrastructure and processes required to make machine learning models available for real time predictions in production environments. Julia provides several powerful approaches for serving models efficiently while maintaining reliability and scalability.

The fundamental architecture of model serving typically involves exposing models through APIs that accept input data and return predictions. Julia's HTTP.jl and related packages enable building robust REST APIs with proper request handling and response formatting. Production serving systems should implement proper input validation, request logging, and error handling to ensure reliable operation.

Request handling forms a crucial component of model serving. Input data requires validation and preprocessing before being passed to models, while responses need proper formatting and error handling. Production systems should implement proper request queuing and maintain appropriate timeout policies. Rate limiting may be necessary to prevent resource exhaustion under heavy load.

Performance optimization becomes essential for served models. Julia's compilation capabilities enable efficient execution, while proper batching can improve throughput. Production systems should implement request pooling and maintain proper warm up procedures. Response caching may be appropriate for certain use cases where predictions remain valid across multiple requests.

Scaling strategies need careful consideration in serving architectures. Horizontal scaling through multiple serving instances enables handling increased load, while load balancing ensures even distribution. Production systems should implement proper auto scaling policies and maintain consistent performance across instances. Session affinity may be necessary for certain model types.

Resource management requires careful attention in serving environments. Memory usage patterns should be monitored and controlled, while CPU utilization requires proper allocation. Production systems should implement resource limits and maintain monitoring of usage patterns. Garbage collection tuning may be necessary to maintain consistent latency.

Monitoring capabilities become crucial for served models. Custom metrics should track both technical performance and business metrics, while logging enables detailed analysis. Production systems should implement proper alerting and maintain dashboard visibility. Performance degradation detection enables proactive maintenance of serving infrastructure.

Security considerations require careful implementation. Authentication and authorization control access to prediction endpoints, while encryption protects data in transit. Production systems should implement proper security headers and maintain compliance requirements. Regular security audits ensure ongoing protection of serving infrastructure.

Caching strategies can improve serving performance. Response caching enables reuse of common predictions, while model caching ensures efficient execution. Production systems should implement proper cache invalidation and maintain appropriate cache sizes. Cache warming procedures may be necessary for optimal performance.

Error handling requires robust implementation in serving systems. Proper exception handling ensures graceful failure modes, while retry mechanisms handle transient issues. Production systems should implement circuit breakers and maintain clear error reporting. Fallback strategies enable degraded operation during partial failures.

Version management becomes important for served models. Multiple model versions may need simultaneous serving, while proper routing ensures requests reach appropriate versions. Production systems should implement proper version tracking and maintain compatibility documentation. A/B testing capabilities enable controlled rollout of new versions.

Configuration management requires careful handling in serving environments. Environment specific settings should be properly externalized, while sensitive information requires secure storage. Production systems should implement configuration validation and maintain clear documentation. Version control of configuration ensures traceability of changes.

Health checking capabilities ensure reliable operation. Readiness and liveness probes enable automated monitoring, while custom health metrics track application specific status. Production systems should implement health check endpoints and maintain appropriate thresholds. Automated recovery procedures can handle common failure modes.

Documentation requirements include both technical specifications and operational procedures. Serving documentation should cover API specifications, deployment procedures, and troubleshooting guides. Production systems should maintain proper runbooks and implement clear incident response procedures. Knowledge sharing enables effective operation across team members.

Integration testing becomes essential for served models. Test suites should verify both functional correctness and performance characteristics. Production systems should implement automated deployment testing and maintain proper test coverage. Integration with CI/CD pipelines enables automated validation during updates.

Logging strategies require careful implementation. Structured logging enables efficient analysis, while log levels control verbosity. Production systems should implement log rotation and maintain archival procedures. Log analysis tools enable identifying patterns and troubleshooting issues.

Model serving in Julia combines robust technical capabilities with practical operational considerations. While specific requirements vary across applications, following established patterns and best practices enables building reliable and maintainable serving infrastructure. Regular review and updates ensure continued effectiveness of serving strategies as requirements evolve.

Deployment automation enables consistent and reliable updates to serving infrastructure. Automated deployment scripts handle routine operations, while validation steps ensure proper execution. Production systems should implement deployment verification and maintain rollback capabilities. Blue green deployment strategies enable zero downtime updates.

The choice of serving architecture impacts both performance and maintainability. Synchronous serving through REST APIs enables immediate responses, while asynchronous approaches using message queues support different scaling patterns. Production systems should implement appropriate architectures based on requirements and maintain proper documentation of design decisions.

Resource isolation becomes important in serving environments. Container based deployment provides proper isolation, while resource limits prevent interference between components. Production systems should implement proper container configuration and maintain monitoring of resource usage. Orchestration tools enable managing complex serving deployments.

Chapter 53: Model Monitoring

Model monitoring forms a critical component of maintaining machine learning systems in production environments. As models operate in real world conditions, their performance can degrade over time due to various factors including data drift, concept drift, and changes in underlying patterns. Implementing robust monitoring systems enables early detection of issues and maintains model effectiveness.

Data quality monitoring represents a fundamental aspect of model monitoring. Input data should be continuously validated against expected distributions and patterns. Statistical measures can track feature distributions over time, while automated checks detect anomalies in incoming data. Production systems should maintain historical records of data characteristics and implement alerting when significant deviations occur.

Performance monitoring tracks the ongoing effectiveness of deployed models. Key metrics like accuracy, precision, recall, and business specific KPIs require continuous evaluation. Ground truth collection enables periodic revalidation of model performance. Monitoring systems should track both aggregate metrics and segment specific performance to identify potential issues affecting particular subgroups.

Drift detection forms a crucial component of model monitoring. Feature drift occurs when input distributions change over time, while concept drift represents changes in underlying relationships between features and targets. Statistical tests can identify significant drift patterns, while visualization tools enable understanding drift characteristics. Production systems should implement automated drift detection and maintain appropriate thresholds for alerts.

Resource utilization monitoring ensures efficient operation of serving infrastructure. CPU usage, memory consumption, disk I/O, and network traffic require continuous tracking. Performance metrics like latency and throughput help identify potential bottlenecks. Monitoring systems should maintain historical usage patterns and implement predictive analytics for capacity planning.

Prediction monitoring tracks the characteristics of model outputs over time. Distribution of predictions, confidence scores, and error rates provide insights into model behavior. Unexpected patterns in predictions may indicate underlying issues requiring investigation. Production systems should implement automated analysis of prediction patterns and maintain appropriate alerting thresholds.

Business impact monitoring connects model performance to organizational objectives. Revenue impact, customer satisfaction metrics, and other business KPIs require tracking alongside technical metrics. Cost analysis helps understand the operational expenses of maintaining models in production. Monitoring systems should provide clear visibility into business impact and enable data driven decision making about model updates.

Infrastructure monitoring ensures reliable operation of serving systems. Server health, network connectivity, and dependent services require continuous tracking. System level metrics help identify potential issues before they impact model performance. Production monitoring should implement proper logging of infrastructure events and maintain appropriate backup procedures.

Alert management requires careful implementation in monitoring systems. Alert thresholds should balance sensitivity with practical response capabilities. Alert routing ensures notifications reach appropriate team members, while alert aggregation prevents notification fatigue. Production systems should implement proper alert documentation and maintain clear escalation procedures.

Visualization capabilities enable understanding monitoring data. Dashboards should present key metrics clearly, while detailed views support investigation of specific issues. Time series visualizations help identify trends and patterns in monitoring data. Production systems should implement appropriate visualization tools and maintain proper access controls for monitoring interfaces.

Automated response capabilities can handle common issues. Simple problems may allow automated remediation, while complex issues require human investigation. Circuit breakers can prevent cascade failures, while automated scaling responds to load changes. Production systems should implement appropriate automation and maintain clear documentation of automated responses.

Compliance monitoring ensures adherence to regulatory requirements. Data privacy, model fairness, and other compliance metrics require continuous tracking. Audit logs enable verification of system behavior and compliance status. Production systems should implement appropriate compliance checks and maintain documentation of regulatory requirements.

Historical analysis enables understanding long term patterns. Monitoring data should be retained for appropriate periods, while analysis tools support investigating historical issues. Trend analysis helps identify gradual degradation of model performance. Production systems should implement proper data retention policies and maintain tools for historical analysis.

Integration with existing monitoring infrastructure enables consolidated visibility. Standard monitoring tools can incorporate model specific metrics, while existing alerting systems handle notifications. Common monitoring patterns enable consistent operations across different models. Production systems should implement appropriate integration and maintain documentation of monitoring architecture.

Performance impact of monitoring requires careful consideration. Monitoring overhead should remain minimal, while ensuring collection of necessary metrics. Sampling strategies can reduce monitoring load while maintaining statistical validity. Production systems should implement efficient monitoring and maintain appropriate resource allocation for monitoring functions.

Documentation of monitoring systems enables effective operation. Metric definitions, alert thresholds, and response procedures require clear documentation. Runbooks should cover common issues and troubleshooting approaches. Production systems should maintain updated documentation and implement knowledge sharing across team members.

Model monitoring in Julia combines technical capabilities with operational requirements. While specific monitoring needs vary across applications, implementing comprehensive monitoring enables maintaining effective models in production. Regular review and updates ensure monitoring systems continue meeting evolving requirements.

Testing monitoring systems ensures reliable operation. Test cases should verify metric collection, alerting functionality, and automated responses. Integration testing validates interaction with existing monitoring infrastructure. Production systems should implement monitoring tests and maintain appropriate test coverage.

Monitoring configuration requires careful management. Threshold values, retention periods, and other settings should be properly externalized. Configuration changes require appropriate review and validation. Production systems should implement configuration management and maintain proper version control of monitoring settings.

The effectiveness of model monitoring directly impacts the ongoing value of machine learning systems. Regular evaluation of monitoring effectiveness enables continuous improvement of monitoring strategies. Production systems should implement periodic reviews and maintain appropriate updates to monitoring approaches as requirements evolve.

Chapter 54: Case Study: Financial Analytics

In this chapter, we explore a comprehensive case study of implementing Julia for financial analytics in a production environment. Financial analytics presents unique challenges requiring both high performance computing and robust data processing capabilities, making it an ideal showcase for Julia's strengths.

Let's begin with a real world scenario from a quantitative trading firm that transitioned their analytics pipeline from Python to Julia. The firm processes market data from multiple exchanges, performs real time risk calculations, and executes automated trading strategies. Their previous Python based system struggled with processing latency and scaling challenges during high volume periods.

The initial implementation focused on market data processing. Julia's multiple dispatch system proved particularly valuable for handling different data formats from various exchanges. Custom types were defined for each exchange's data structure, with common processing interfaces implemented through multiple dispatch. This approach provided both type safety and high performance, while maintaining clean, maintainable code.

```julia
struct NYSEData
timestamp::DateTime
symbol::String
price::Float64
volume::Int64
end
struct NASDAQData
time::DateTime
ticker::String
```

```
last::Float64
size::Int64
end
function process_trade(data::NYSEData)
# NYSE specific processing
end
function process_trade(data::NASDAQData)
# NASDAQ specific processing
end
```

Performance improvements were immediately apparent. The Julia implementation reduced average processing latency from 50 milliseconds to under 5 milliseconds, primarily due to Julia's efficient memory management and compilation optimizations. The system handled peak loads of over 100,000 messages per second without degradation.

Risk calculations presented another significant challenge. The previous Python implementation relied heavily on NumPy for vector operations and Pandas for time series analysis. The Julia implementation leveraged native array operations and the TimeArrays.jl package, achieving both cleaner code and better performance. Complex risk calculations that previously took several seconds were completed in milliseconds.

Statistical arbitrage strategies benefited particularly from Julia's mathematical capabilities. The LinearAlgebra standard library provided efficient implementations of covariance calculations and matrix operations. Custom optimization routines implemented in Julia showed order of magnitude improvements over Python equivalents, enabling more sophisticated trading strategies.

Data persistence and retrieval posed interesting challenges. The team implemented a custom time series database using Julia's memory mapping capabilities, providing near real time access to historical data.

Integration with existing PostgreSQL databases was handled through LibPQ.jl, with custom types ensuring type safety throughout the data pipeline.

```julia
struct TradeRecord
timestamp::DateTime
symbol::String
price::Float64
volume::Int64
exchange::String
end
function store_trade(record::TradeRecord)
# Custom time series storage implementation
end
function retrieve_trades(symbol::String, start_time::DateTime,
end_time::DateTime)
# Efficient historical data retrieval
end
```

Distributed computing capabilities proved crucial for handling large scale backtesting. Julia's built in distributed computing features enabled parallel execution across multiple machines with minimal code changes. The team implemented a custom task scheduler that distributed backtesting jobs while maintaining careful control over memory usage.

Real time visualization requirements were met using Plots.jl with the WebIO backend, providing interactive dashboards for traders. Custom plotting recipes enabled efficient visualization of large datasets, while Julia's compilation ensured smooth updates even with rapidly changing data.

Error handling and system reliability required careful consideration. The team implemented comprehensive logging using the Logging standard library, with custom log handlers for different severity levels. Circuit breakers and automatic failover mechanisms were implemented to handle exchange connectivity issues and other potential failures.

```julia
function execute_trade(order::Order)
try
result = submit_to_exchange(order)
@info "Trade executed" order_id=order.id result=result
return result
catch e
@error "Trade execution failed" order=order exception=e
rethrow(e)
end
end
```

Performance monitoring was implemented using custom metrics collection and the StatsBase package for statistical analysis. The system tracked various performance indicators including message latency, processing times, and memory usage. Regular benchmarking ensured continued performance as the system evolved.

Security considerations were paramount given the financial nature of the system. The team implemented comprehensive audit logging, encryption of sensitive data, and fine grained access controls. Julia's type system helped enforce security constraints at the code level.

Integration with existing systems required careful planning. The team developed custom interfaces to existing risk management systems, using JSON.jl for data interchange. RESTful APIs were implemented using HTTP.jl, providing external access to specific system capabilities.

Deployment and scaling procedures were standardized using Docker containers. The team developed custom build scripts that created optimized container images including precompiled Julia code.

Kubernetes orchestration managed container deployment and scaling based on load.

The migration process took several months, with different components transitioned incrementally. The team maintained careful performance comparisons throughout the process, documenting improvements and addressing any regressions. The final system showed consistent performance improvements ranging from 5x to 20x depending on the specific operation.

Maintenance procedures were established including regular code reviews, performance testing, and system health checks. The team developed comprehensive documentation covering both technical details and operational procedures. Regular training sessions ensured team members remained proficient with Julia development.

The success of this implementation demonstrated Julia's capabilities for high performance financial analytics. Key factors in the success included Julia's multiple dispatch system, efficient numerical computing capabilities, and strong type system. The ability to write high performance code while maintaining clarity and maintainability proved particularly valuable.

This case study illustrates how Julia can transform financial analytics workflows, providing both performance improvements and better code organization. The lessons learned include the importance of careful planning, incremental migration, and comprehensive testing. The resulting system provided a solid foundation for future expansion and enhancement.

Chapter 55: Case Study: Bioinformatics

In this chapter, we explore the application of Julia in bioinformatics, focusing on real world implementations in genomic data analysis and computational biology. Bioinformatics presents unique computational challenges due to massive datasets, complex algorithms, and the need for reproducible research.

We begin with a case study from a genomics research institute that migrated their DNA sequence analysis pipeline from Python and R to Julia. The institute processes thousands of genome sequences daily, performing various analyses including sequence alignment, variant calling, and phylogenetic tree construction. Their previous workflow involved multiple tools and languages, creating bottlenecks in data processing and analysis.

The first challenge addressed was sequence data processing. Julia's efficient string manipulation capabilities and binary data handling proved invaluable for processing FASTQ files. The team developed custom types for representing sequence data, leveraging Julia's type system to ensure data integrity throughout the pipeline.

```julia
struct DNASequence
identifier::String
sequence::String
quality_scores::Vector{Int8}
metadata::Dict{String, Any}
end
struct SequenceAlignment
reference::DNASequence
query::DNASequence
score::Float64
alignment_positions::Vector{Tuple{Int, Int}}
end
```

Performance gains were substantial. The Julia implementation processed raw sequence files approximately 8 times faster than the previous Python based solution. Memory usage was also significantly reduced through careful type design and efficient algorithms.

Sequence alignment presented another significant challenge. The team implemented custom alignment algorithms using Julia's native array operations and parallel computing capabilities. The resulting implementation not only matched the speed of specialized C++ tools but provided greater flexibility for algorithm modification and enhancement.

Variant calling workflows demonstrated Julia's strength in statistical computing. The team implemented probabilistic models for variant detection using Distributions.jl and StatsFuns.jl. Custom statistical tests were implemented with better performance than equivalent R implementations while maintaining similar syntax and usability.

Phylogenetic analysis showcased Julia's capabilities for complex computational tasks. Tree construction algorithms were implemented using Julia's graph libraries and optimization tools. The resulting implementation handled larger datasets than previously possible, enabling analysis of evolutionary relationships across thousands of sequences simultaneously.

Data visualization requirements were met through a combination of Plots.jl and BioSequences.jl. Custom plotting recipes were developed for common bioinformatics visualizations including sequence logos, coverage plots, and phylogenetic trees. Interactive visualizations were implemented using Pluto.jl notebooks, enabling researchers to explore results dynamically.

The team developed custom parsers for common bioinformatics file formats including FASTA, GenBank, and VCF files. Julia's metaprogramming capabilities enabled generation of efficient parsing code while maintaining clear syntax. File handling performance improved significantly compared to Python's BioPython library.

```julia
function parse_fasta(filename::String)
sequences = Vector{DNASequence}()
current_header = ""
current_sequence = ""
for line in eachline(filename)
if startswith(line, '>')
if !isempty(current_sequence)
push!(sequences, DNASequence(current_header, current_sequence))
end
current_header = strip(line[2:end])
current_sequence = ""
else
current_sequence *= strip(line)
end
end
if !isempty(current_sequence)
push!(sequences, DNASequence(current_header, current_sequence))
end
return sequences
end
```

Distributed computing proved essential for handling large scale analyses. The team implemented parallel processing patterns for computationally intensive tasks like multiple sequence alignment and phylogenetic inference. Julia's built in distributed computing capabilities simplified the implementation of parallel algorithms.

Integration with existing bioinformatics tools was achieved through Julia's excellent interoperability features. The team developed interfaces to popular tools like BLAST and HMMER using Julia's process management capabilities. Results were seamlessly integrated into the Julia based workflow while maintaining high performance.

Database integration posed unique challenges due to the size and complexity of genomic data. The team implemented custom database solutions using both SQL and NoSQL approaches, with Julia's type system ensuring data consistency. Connection pooling and efficient query generation improved database performance significantly.

The pipeline included comprehensive quality control measures. Statistical analyses were implemented to detect sequencing artifacts and potential contamination. Results were automatically logged and flagged for review when quality metrics fell outside acceptable ranges.

Reproducibility was ensured through careful version control of both code and data. The team developed custom tools for tracking analysis parameters and intermediate results. Docker containers were used to package the entire analysis environment, ensuring consistent results across different systems.

```julia
struct AnalysisMetadata
timestamp::DateTime
parameters::Dict{String, Any}
input_files::Vector{String}
software_versions::Dict{String, VersionNumber}
environment_hash::String
end
```

Performance monitoring was implemented throughout the pipeline. Custom benchmarking tools tracked processing time and resource usage for each analysis step. Regular performance reviews identified bottlenecks and guided optimization efforts.

The system included comprehensive error handling and recovery mechanisms. Failed analyses were automatically retried with appropriate backoff periods. Detailed error logging helped identify systematic issues and guided pipeline improvements.

Documentation was prioritized throughout development. The team maintained extensive documentation covering both usage and implementation details. Regular workshops ensured all team members understood both the biological and computational aspects of the system.

The migration process occurred over several months, with different components transitioned incrementally. Careful validation ensured results matched or exceeded the accuracy of previous implementations. The final system showed performance improvements ranging from 5x to 15x depending on the specific analysis.

This case study demonstrates Julia's effectiveness for bioinformatics applications. Key success factors included Julia's performance, type system, and ability to handle complex algorithms clearly and efficiently. The resulting system provided a solid foundation for future genomics research while improving productivity and reducing computational resources needed.

The lessons learned include the importance of careful type design, effective use of parallel computing, and maintaining biological relevance while pursuing performance improvements. The success of this implementation suggests Julia could play an increasingly important role in bioinformatics as the field continues to grow in both data volume and computational complexity.

Chapter 56: Case Study: IoT Data Processing

In this chapter, we explore how Julia can be effectively utilized for processing and analyzing Internet of Things (IoT) data through a real world case study of a smart manufacturing facility. IoT data processing presents unique challenges due to high velocity data streams, the need for real time analytics, and complex sensor data integration requirements.

The case study follows a manufacturing company that implemented a Julia based system to monitor and analyze data from thousands of sensors across their production lines. Their previous system, built with Python, struggled to handle the volume and velocity of incoming data, leading to delays in detecting critical equipment issues.

The first challenge addressed was data ingestion. The team developed a high performance message queue system using Julia's asynchronous programming capabilities. This system handled multiple protocols including MQTT and AMQP, processing millions of messages per minute from various sensors.

```julia
struct SensorReading
sensor_id::String
timestamp::DateTime
value::Float64
metadata::Dict{String, Any}
quality_flags::BitVector
end
struct DataStream
stream_id::String
readings::Channel{SensorReading}
```

```
processing_config::Dict{String, Any}
end
```

Real time processing requirements were met through careful implementation of stream processing patterns. The team developed a custom stream processing framework that handled data validation, transformation, and preliminary analysis with minimal latency. Julia's multiple dispatch system proved valuable for handling different sensor types and data formats efficiently.

Time series analysis played a crucial role in the system. The team implemented various algorithms for anomaly detection, trend analysis, and predictive maintenance. Julia's native support for complex mathematical operations enabled sophisticated analysis without sacrificing performance.

Data quality management was implemented throughout the processing pipeline. The system automatically detected sensor malfunctions, communication issues, and data anomalies. Custom validation rules were implemented for different sensor types, ensuring data reliability.

```julia
function validate_sensor_reading(reading::SensorReading, rules::ValidationRules)
flags = BitVector(undef, length(rules))
for (i, rule) in enumerate(rules)
flags[i] = check_rule(reading, rule)
end
return flags
end
```

Edge computing capabilities were developed to reduce network load and enable faster response times. Julia's excellent performance on resource constrained devices allowed sophisticated processing at the edge, with only relevant data transmitted to central systems.

The team implemented sophisticated data aggregation mechanisms to handle the high volume of incoming data. Time based windows and custom aggregation functions enabled efficient storage while maintaining analytical value. Julia's type system ensured consistent handling of different aggregation scenarios.

Machine learning models were integrated for predictive maintenance and quality control. The team used MLJ.jl to implement various models including random forests and neural networks. Online learning capabilities were developed to continuously update models based on new data.

Visualization requirements were addressed through a combination of static and real time plotting. The team developed custom dashboards using Plots.jl and various web frameworks. Interactive visualizations enabled operators to explore data and investigate anomalies effectively.

Database integration posed significant challenges due to the volume of data. The team implemented a tiered storage strategy, using time series databases for recent data and compressed archives for historical data. Custom database adapters optimized for IoT data patterns improved query performance significantly.

The system included comprehensive monitoring and alerting capabilities. Custom alert rules were implemented based on both simple thresholds and complex pattern matching. Julia's performance enabled sophisticated real time monitoring without significant overhead.

```julia
struct AlertRule
rule_id::String
condition::Function
severity::Symbol
action::Function
```

```
cooldown::Period
end
function check_alerts(reading::SensorReading, rules::Vector{AlertRule})
triggered_alerts = AlertRule[]
for rule in rules
if rule.condition(reading)
push!(triggered_alerts, rule)
end
end
return triggered_alerts
end
```

Distributed computing was essential for handling the scale of data processing. The team implemented both vertical and horizontal scaling strategies, utilizing Julia's built in distributed computing capabilities. Load balancing mechanisms ensured efficient resource utilization across the processing cluster.

Integration with existing manufacturing systems was achieved through custom interfaces and protocols. The team developed adapters for various industrial control systems and enterprise software. Julia's flexibility in handling different data formats and protocols simplified integration efforts.

Security was a primary concern throughout development. The team implemented comprehensive security measures including encryption, authentication, and access control. Regular security audits ensured the system met industrial security standards.

Performance optimization was an ongoing process. The team developed custom profiling tools to identify bottlenecks and optimize critical paths. Regular performance reviews guided system improvements and resource allocation.

Error handling and recovery mechanisms were implemented throughout the system. Failed processing tasks were automatically retried with appropriate backoff strategies. Detailed error logging helped identify systematic issues and guided improvements.

Documentation was maintained covering both technical details and operational procedures. Regular training sessions ensured operators and maintenance staff could effectively use and troubleshoot the system.

The migration from the previous Python based system occurred gradually over several months. Careful validation ensured no critical data was lost during the transition. The final system showed performance improvements of over 20x in key processing tasks.

This case study demonstrates Julia's effectiveness for IoT data processing applications. Key success factors included Julia's performance, ability to handle real time processing, and excellent support for numerical computing. The resulting system provided a robust foundation for industrial IoT applications while significantly improving processing efficiency and analytical capabilities.

The lessons learned include the importance of careful system architecture, effective use of Julia's type system, and maintaining balance between real time processing requirements and analytical depth. The success of this implementation suggests Julia could play an increasingly important role in industrial IoT applications as manufacturing systems become more data intensive.

Chapter 57: Case Study: Computer Vision

Chapter 57 focuses on a practical case study demonstrating Julia's capabilities in computer vision applications through the example of an automated quality control system for a manufacturing production line. This real world implementation showcases how Julia's performance and ecosystem can be leveraged for industrial computer vision tasks.

The case study follows a manufacturing company that needed to implement high speed visual inspection of products on their assembly line. Their existing Python based solution couldn't keep up with production speeds, leading to missed defects and production bottlenecks. The transition to Julia dramatically improved processing speed and accuracy.

The first challenge was implementing efficient image acquisition and preprocessing. The team developed a high performance image capture system using Julia's interface with industrial cameras. The system handled multiple camera streams simultaneously, processing thousands of frames per second.

```julia
struct ImageFrame
timestamp::DateTime
image::Array{UInt8, 3}
camera_id::String
metadata::Dict{String, Any}
end
function preprocess_frame(frame::ImageFrame)
img = frame.image
# Basic preprocessing operations
img = adjust_contrast(img)
img = denoise(img)
img = normalize(img)
```

```
return img
end
```

Image preprocessing utilized Julia's native array operations and specialized image processing libraries. The team implemented custom preprocessing pipelines optimized for their specific use case, including contrast adjustment, noise reduction, and normalization. Julia's performance with array operations proved particularly valuable for these tasks.

Feature extraction was a critical component of the system. The team implemented various computer vision algorithms including edge detection, blob analysis, and texture feature extraction. Julia's multiple dispatch system enabled efficient implementation of different feature extraction strategies for different product types.

The core defect detection system used a combination of traditional computer vision techniques and deep learning models. The team utilized Flux.jl to implement custom convolutional neural networks for defect classification. Transfer learning was employed to reduce training data requirements while maintaining high accuracy.

```julia
struct DefectDetector
feature_extractor::Chain
classifier::Chain
preprocessing::Function
confidence_threshold::Float64
end
function detect_defects(image::Array{Float32, 3}, detector::DefectDetector)
preprocessed = detector.preprocessing(image)
features = detector.feature_extractor(preprocessed)
predictions = detector.classifier(features)
```

```
    return process_predictions(predictions, detector.confidence_threshold)
    end
```

Real time performance requirements posed significant challenges. The team implemented various optimization techniques including GPU acceleration through CUDA.jl for neural network inference. Careful memory management and buffer strategies ensured consistent performance under sustained load.

The system included sophisticated calibration and registration capabilities. Automatic camera calibration routines compensated for lens distortion and ensured accurate measurements. Multi camera registration enabled comprehensive product inspection from multiple angles.

Quality metrics tracking was implemented throughout the system. The team developed custom metrics for detection accuracy, processing speed, and system reliability. Continuous monitoring of these metrics guided system improvements and maintenance schedules.

Visualization capabilities were essential for system operation and debugging. The team implemented both real time visualization of processing results and tools for detailed analysis of detected defects. Custom visualization components helped operators understand and verify system decisions.

Integration with the manufacturing execution system posed several challenges. The team developed robust interfaces for exchanging data with production control systems and quality management databases. Real time feedback enabled immediate production adjustments based on inspection results.

Error handling and system reliability were critical concerns. The team implemented comprehensive error recovery mechanisms and fallback procedures. Watchdog processes monitored system health and initiated recovery procedures when necessary.

```julia
struct SystemStatus
components::Dict{String, Bool}
performance_metrics::Dict{String, Float64}
error_counts::Dict{String, Int}
last_check::DateTime
end
function monitor_system_health(status::SystemStatus)
if any(values(status.error_counts) .> error_thresholds)
initiate_recovery_procedure(status)
end
end
```

Data management strategies were developed to handle the large volume of image data. The team implemented efficient storage and retrieval mechanisms for both raw images and processing results. Automated data retention policies balanced storage requirements with analytical needs.

The system included extensive logging and debugging capabilities. Detailed logs of system operation, detection results, and error conditions supported both immediate troubleshooting and long term system improvement.

Performance optimization was an ongoing process. The team used Julia's profiling tools to identify and eliminate bottlenecks. Regular performance reviews guided system tuning and hardware allocation decisions.

Training and documentation were crucial for system adoption. The team developed comprehensive documentation covering system operation, maintenance procedures, and troubleshooting guides. Regular operator training ensured effective system utilization.

The migration from the previous system was carefully managed to minimize production impact. Parallel operation of old and new systems enabled thorough validation before full cutover. The final system showed detection accuracy improvements of 15% while processing images 30x faster than the previous solution.

This case study demonstrates Julia's effectiveness for industrial computer vision applications. Key success factors included Julia's performance with array operations, GPU computing capabilities, and extensive image processing libraries. The resulting system provided robust visual inspection capabilities while meeting demanding industrial performance requirements.

The lessons learned include the importance of careful algorithm selection, effective use of Julia's performance features, and maintaining balance between processing speed and detection accuracy. The success of this implementation suggests Julia could be particularly valuable for industrial computer vision applications requiring high performance and sophisticated image analysis capabilities.

Chapter 58: Performance Tuning for Big Data

When dealing with big data applications in Julia, performance tuning becomes critical for maintaining system efficiency and responsiveness. This chapter explores comprehensive strategies and techniques for optimizing Julia applications that process large scale datasets, focusing on both computational and memory efficiency.

Performance tuning for big data applications starts with proper data structures and access patterns. When working with large datasets, choosing the right data structure can significantly impact performance. Julia's built in array types offer excellent performance for many operations, but specialized data structures may be more appropriate for specific use cases. For instance, sparse arrays can dramatically reduce memory usage and improve computation speed when dealing with sparse data.

Memory management becomes particularly crucial when handling big data. Julia's garbage collector performs well in most situations, but understanding and optimizing memory allocation patterns can lead to substantial performance improvements. Pre allocation of arrays and careful management of temporary objects can significantly reduce garbage collection overhead.

```julia
function process_large_dataset(data)
# Pre allocate result arrays
results = Vector{Float64}(undef, size(data, 1))
buffer = similar(data, size(data, 2))
for i in axes(data, 1)
# Reuse buffer instead of creating new allocations
compute_result!(view(results, i), view(data, i, :), buffer)
end
```

```
results
end
```

Data loading and preprocessing strategies play a vital role in big data performance. Implementing efficient data loading mechanisms, such as memory mapping for large files or streaming processing for continuous data sources, can prevent memory bottlenecks. Chunked processing allows handling datasets larger than available RAM by processing data in manageable portions.

Parallelization strategies must be carefully considered for big data applications. Julia offers multiple approaches to parallel processing, including multi threading, distributed computing, and GPU acceleration. The choice of parallelization strategy depends on factors such as data size, computation type, and available hardware resources.

Multi threading often provides the simplest path to improved performance for data parallel operations. Julia's built in threading primitives make it straightforward to parallelize computations across available CPU cores. However, care must be taken to avoid thread contention and ensure proper load balancing.

```julia
function parallel_process_chunks(data)
n_chunks = nthreads()
chunk_size = ceil(Int, size(data, 1) / n_chunks)
results = zeros(size(data, 1))
@threads for i in 1:n_chunks
start_idx = (i-1) * chunk_size + 1
end_idx = min(i * chunk_size, size(data, 1))
process_chunk!(view(results, start_idx:end_idx), view(data, start_idx:end_idx, :))
end
results
end
```

```
```

Distributed computing becomes essential when dataset sizes exceed single machine capacity. Julia's distributed computing capabilities allow spreading computation across multiple nodes. Effective use of distributed computing requires careful consideration of data partitioning and communication patterns to minimize overhead.

GPU acceleration can provide dramatic speedups for certain types of computations, particularly those involving linear algebra or other highly parallel operations. CUDA.jl and related packages enable leveraging GPU hardware for big data processing, though careful attention must be paid to data transfer overhead.

I/O optimization is crucial for big data applications. Implementing efficient data serialization and deserialization mechanisms, using appropriate file formats, and optimizing database queries can significantly impact overall system performance. Memory mapped files often provide an excellent balance between performance and memory usage for large datasets.

Query optimization becomes particularly important when working with big data. Whether using DataFrames.jl or database queries, understanding and optimizing query patterns can lead to substantial performance improvements. This includes proper indexing, query planning, and minimizing unnecessary data movement.

```julia
function optimized_query(df::DataFrame, conditions)
# Use indices where available
indexed_result = @view df[df.index .∈ conditions, :]
# Process in chunks to control memory usage
chunk_size = 1_000_000
results = Vector{Float64}()
for chunk in Iterators.partition(1:nrow(indexed_result), chunk_size)
chunk_result = process_chunk(view(indexed_result, chunk, :))
```

```
        append!(results, chunk_result)
    end
    results
end
```

Caching strategies can significantly improve performance for big data applications. This includes both in memory caching for frequently accessed data and disk based caching for intermediate results. Implementing effective cache invalidation and update strategies is crucial for maintaining data consistency.

Performance monitoring and profiling become even more critical with big data applications. Regular profiling helps identify bottlenecks and guides optimization efforts. Julia's built in profiling tools, combined with custom performance metrics, provide valuable insights into system behavior under load.

Resource management strategies must be carefully considered. This includes managing memory usage, controlling CPU utilization, and balancing I/O operations. Implementing appropriate resource limits and monitoring helps prevent system overload and ensures consistent performance.

Error handling and recovery mechanisms need special attention in big data applications. Implementing robust error handling, including appropriate retry mechanisms and fallback strategies, helps maintain system reliability when processing large datasets.

Optimization for specific hardware architectures can provide significant performance improvements. This includes taking advantage of CPU vector instructions, optimizing memory access patterns for specific cache architectures, and leveraging specialized hardware accelerators when available.

Documentation and monitoring of performance characteristics becomes crucial for big data applications. Maintaining detailed performance metrics, including processing times, resource utilization, and error rates, helps track system health and guide optimization efforts.

The chapter concludes with a discussion of performance testing and validation strategies for big data applications. This includes developing appropriate test datasets, implementing performance benchmarks, and establishing performance criteria for production deployment.

Success in performance tuning big data applications requires a systematic approach combining multiple optimization strategies. Regular monitoring, profiling, and incremental optimization ensure systems maintain high performance as data volumes and processing requirements grow.

Chapter 59: Scaling Julia Applications

Here's Chapter 59 on Scaling Julia Applications:

Scaling Julia applications from prototype to production requires careful consideration of architecture, resource management, and system design principles. This chapter explores comprehensive strategies for building scalable Julia applications that can handle growing data volumes, user loads, and computational demands while maintaining performance and reliability.

Vertical scaling, or scaling up, involves adding more resources to existing machines. Julia applications can effectively utilize additional CPU cores through multi threading and additional memory through proper memory management. When scaling vertically, it's crucial to understand how your application utilizes these resources and ensure that the codebase can effectively leverage additional capacity.

```julia
function configure_threading(computation_type)
# Adjust number of BLAS threads based on workload
BLAS.set_num_threads(min(8, Sys.CPU_THREADS))
# Configure thread pool for application specific tasks
if computation_type == :cpu_intensive
ENV["JULIA_NUM_THREADS"] = Sys.CPU_THREADS
else
ENV["JULIA_NUM_THREADS"] =
div(Sys.CPU_THREADS, 2)
end
end
```

Horizontal scaling, or scaling out, involves distributing computation across multiple machines. Julia's distributed computing capabilities provide several approaches to horizontal scaling. The Distributed.jl package enables creating clusters of Julia processes that can work together on computational tasks. When implementing horizontal scaling, careful consideration must be given to data partitioning, communication patterns, and fault tolerance.

Load balancing becomes critical when scaling horizontally. Implementing effective load balancing strategies ensures work is distributed evenly across available resources. This might involve dynamic work distribution, worker pools, or specialized scheduling algorithms depending on the application requirements.

```julia
function distribute_workload(tasks, workers)
# Create a worker pool
pool = WorkerPool(workers)
# Distribute tasks with load balancing
results = Vector{Future}(undef, length(tasks))
for (i, task) in enumerate(tasks)
results[i] = remote_call(next_worker(pool)) do
process_task(task)
end
end
fetch.(results)
end
```

Data partitioning strategies play a crucial role in scalable applications. Effective partitioning ensures data is distributed appropriately across available resources while minimizing communication overhead. This might involve range partitioning, hash partitioning, or more sophisticated schemes based on application specific requirements.

Stateless design principles become increasingly important as applications scale. Minimizing shared state and implementing appropriate synchronization mechanisms helps prevent bottlenecks and ensures system reliability. When state must be shared, consider using distributed key value stores or database systems designed for scalability.

Service discovery and coordination become essential components of scaled applications. Tools like ZooKeeper or etcd can be integrated with Julia applications to manage service discovery, configuration, and coordination across distributed components. This becomes particularly important in microservices architectures or distributed systems.

Caching strategies must evolve as applications scale. This might involve implementing distributed caching solutions, cache hierarchies, or sophisticated cache invalidation protocols. The choice of caching strategy depends on factors such as data access patterns, consistency requirements, and performance goals.

```julia
struct DistributedCache
local_cache::Dict{String, Any}
remote_cache::RedisConnection
ttl::Int64
function DistributedCache(redis_url, ttl=3600)
new(Dict{String, Any}(), Redis.connect(redis_url), ttl)
end
end
function get_cached_value(cache::DistributedCache, key)
# Check local cache first
haskey(cache.local_cache, key) && return cache.local_cache[key]
# Check distributed cache
value = get(cache.remote_cache, key)
isnothing(value) && return nothing
# Update local cache
cache.local_cache[key] = value
value
end
```

Message queuing systems often become necessary for handling asynchronous processing in scaled applications. Julia can integrate with message brokers like RabbitMQ or Apache Kafka to implement reliable message passing and event driven architectures. This enables building loosely coupled, scalable system components.

Database scaling strategies must be considered as data volumes grow. This might involve implementing database sharding, read replicas, or migration to distributed database systems. Julia's database interfaces can work with various database scaling approaches while maintaining application performance.

Monitoring and observability become more complex in scaled applications. Implementing comprehensive monitoring solutions that can track system health, performance metrics, and resource utilization across distributed components is crucial. This might involve integrating with monitoring platforms or implementing custom monitoring solutions.

Error handling and resilience patterns must be adapted for scaled applications. This includes implementing circuit breakers, retry mechanisms, and fallback strategies that work effectively across distributed systems. Proper error handling becomes particularly important when dealing with network partitions or component failures.

```julia
function resilient_operation(operation, max_retries=3)
retries = 0
while retries < max_retries
try
return operation()
catch e
retries += 1
if retries == max_retries
rethrow(e)
```

```
end
# Exponential backoff
sleep(2^retries)
end
end
end
```

Resource management becomes more sophisticated in scaled applications. This includes implementing resource pools, connection management, and appropriate resource cleanup mechanisms. Proper resource management helps prevent resource leaks and ensures system stability under load.

Security considerations must scale with the application. This includes implementing appropriate authentication and authorization mechanisms that work across distributed components, securing communication channels, and maintaining proper access controls as the system grows.

Deployment strategies must evolve to support scaled applications. This might involve implementing rolling deployments, blue green deployments, or canary releases. Proper deployment strategies help maintain system availability while updating components.

Configuration management becomes more complex in scaled applications. Implementing centralized configuration management, feature flags, and dynamic configuration updates helps maintain system flexibility while ensuring consistency across components.

The chapter concludes with a discussion of scaling patterns and anti patterns, providing guidance on common pitfalls to avoid and best practices to follow when scaling Julia applications. Success in scaling requires careful attention to system architecture, resource management, and operational considerations while maintaining code quality and system reliability.

Chapter 60: Production Deployment Checklist

Here's Chapter 60 on Production Deployment Checklist:

Moving a Julia application from development to production requires careful attention to numerous details to ensure reliability, security, and performance. This comprehensive checklist provides a systematic approach to preparing and validating your Julia application for production deployment.

Code Quality and Documentation represents the foundation of a production ready application. Ensure all code follows consistent style guidelines, preferably using JuliaFormatter.jl for automated formatting. Documentation should include detailed API references, architecture diagrams, and deployment instructions. Code comments should explain complex algorithms and business logic rather than obvious operations. Verify that all public functions have docstrings with examples and clear parameter descriptions.

Performance optimization must be verified before deployment. Run comprehensive benchmarks using BenchmarkTools.jl to identify potential bottlenecks. Profile the application under expected production loads to ensure acceptable performance characteristics. Verify that memory usage remains stable during extended operation periods. Consider implementing performance monitoring hooks to track runtime behavior.

Testing coverage should be extensive and automated. Unit tests should cover all critical code paths and edge cases. Integration tests should verify system component interactions. End to end tests should validate complete business workflows. Load tests should confirm system behavior under stress. All tests should pass consistently in the deployment environment. Consider implementing smoke tests that run immediately after deployment to verify basic functionality.

```julia
function deployment_test_suite()
@testset "Pre deployment Validation" begin
@testset "Unit Tests" run_unit_tests()
@testset "Integration Tests" run_integration_tests()
@testset "Performance Tests" run_performance_tests()
@testset "Load Tests" run_load_tests()
end
end
```

Dependency management requires careful attention. Lock all package versions using Manifest.toml to ensure reproducible deployments. Audit dependencies for security vulnerabilities using automated tools. Verify that all required system libraries are documented and included in deployment instructions. Consider creating a containerized deployment to manage dependencies consistently.

Configuration management should be environment aware. Implement configuration validation to catch errors early. Use environment variables for sensitive configuration values. Consider using a configuration management service for dynamic settings. Document all configuration options and their impact. Implement feature flags for gradual rollout of new functionality.

Error handling must be comprehensive and production grade. Implement proper exception handling throughout the application. Set up error reporting to capture stack traces and relevant context. Configure appropriate logging levels for different environments. Implement retry logic for transient failures. Consider circuit breakers for external service calls.

Security considerations must be thoroughly addressed. Implement proper authentication and authorization mechanisms. Encrypt sensitive data both in transit and at rest. Configure secure communication channels using TLS. Implement rate limiting for public endpoints. Regular security audits should be performed. Consider automated security scanning tools.

Monitoring and observability infrastructure must be in place. Configure comprehensive logging with appropriate detail levels. Implement metrics collection for key performance indicators. Set up alerting for critical conditions. Configure distributed tracing if applicable. Ensure logs are properly rotated and archived.

```julia
function configure_monitoring()
# Configure logging
logger = SimpleLogger(LogLevel(INFO))
global_logger(logger)
# Initialize metrics collection
metrics = init_metrics_collector()
# Configure health checks
health_checks = [
DatabaseHealthCheck(),
CacheHealthCheck(),
APIHealthCheck()
]
# Setup alerting
configure_alerts(metrics, health_checks)
end
```

Backup and recovery procedures must be documented and tested. Implement automated backup solutions for critical data. Document and test restore procedures. Verify backup integrity regularly. Implement disaster recovery plans and test them periodically.

Resource management should be properly configured. Set appropriate connection pool sizes for databases and external services. Configure worker pools and thread counts optimally. Implement proper resource cleanup mechanisms. Monitor resource utilization and implement auto scaling if needed.

Deployment automation should be fully implemented. Create automated deployment scripts or pipelines. Implement rollback procedures for failed deployments. Consider blue green deployment strategies. Document deployment procedures completely. Test deployment procedures in staging environment.

Health checks and readiness probes should be implemented. Create endpoints for kubernetes or load balancer health checks. Implement readiness checks for application startup. Configure liveness probes to detect deadlocks or hanging processes. Implement circuit breakers for external dependencies.

Load balancing and scaling configuration should be verified. Configure appropriate scaling thresholds. Implement proper load balancing strategies. Test auto scaling behavior under load. Verify session handling in distributed environments.

Database optimization should be completed. Verify index optimization for common queries. Implement connection pooling appropriately. Configure query timeouts and retry logic. Implement database failover procedures if applicable.

Cache configuration should be optimized. Implement appropriate cache invalidation strategies. Configure cache sizes and eviction policies. Implement distributed caching if needed. Monitor cache hit rates and effectiveness.

API documentation should be complete and accurate. Generate API documentation automatically from code. Implement API versioning strategy. Document rate limits and usage guidelines. Provide API client examples.

Environmental differences should be documented and handled. Account for differences between development and production environments. Document required environment variables. Verify application behavior in all target environments.

Compliance requirements should be addressed. Ensure logging meets compliance requirements. Implement required data retention policies. Document compliance related procedures. Verify privacy policy compliance.

Performance under load should be verified. Conduct load testing under expected production conditions. Verify scaling behavior under stress. Test failure recovery under load. Document performance characteristics and limits.

Finally, create operational procedures and documentation. Document common operational tasks. Create troubleshooting guides. Document incident response procedures. Maintain deployment and configuration history.

This checklist serves as a comprehensive guide, but should be adapted based on specific application requirements and organizational needs. Regular reviews and updates of the deployment checklist help maintain production readiness as the application evolves.

Chapter 61: Troubleshooting Common Issues

Chapter 61 focuses on common issues that developers encounter when working with Julia in production environments and provides systematic approaches to diagnose and resolve these problems.

Memory management issues frequently arise in production Julia applications. One common problem is memory leaks caused by holding onto references longer than necessary, particularly in long running applications. To diagnose these issues, use the memory profiler to track allocations and identify objects that aren't being properly garbage collected. Sometimes this occurs when global variables inadvertently maintain references to large data structures. Converting problematic globals to function local variables often resolves these memory retention issues.

Performance degradation over time represents another frequent challenge. This often manifests as increasing response times or growing memory usage during extended operation. Type instability commonly underlies these problems, particularly when functions encounter unexpected input types in production that weren't encountered during testing. Using @code_warntype to inspect function compilation can reveal these issues. Adding type assertions or restructuring functions to maintain type stability usually resolves the performance degradation.

Database connection issues frequently impact production applications. Connection pools may become exhausted during peak loads, timeouts may occur during network instability, or connections may go stale during periods of low activity. Implementing proper connection pooling with retry logic and connection health checks helps mitigate these issues. Regular monitoring of connection pool metrics helps identify potential problems before they become critical.

Concurrency related bugs often only surface under production loads. Race conditions, deadlocks, and thread safety issues can be particularly challenging to diagnose. Using logging with thread IDs and distributed tracing helps track down these issues. Careful use of synchronization primitives and message passing patterns can prevent many concurrency problems. The ThreadSafety.jl package can help identify potential thread safety issues during development.

Configuration related problems commonly occur when moving between environments. Environment variables may be missing or have incorrect values, configuration files may have permission issues, or secret management services may be unreachable. Implementing strict configuration validation at startup helps catch these issues early. Using a configuration management service with proper access control and audit logging helps track down configuration related problems.

Network related issues often impact distributed Julia applications. Service discovery may fail, network latency may exceed timeouts, or DNS resolution may fail intermittently. Implementing circuit breakers and fallback mechanisms helps maintain partial functionality during network issues. Proper monitoring of network metrics and latency helps identify potential problems early.

Resource exhaustion represents another common category of production issues. CPU cores may become saturated, available memory may run low, or disk space may be consumed faster than expected. Implementing resource monitoring and alerting helps catch these issues before they become critical. Automatic scaling policies can help manage resource utilization, while cleanup jobs can manage disk space usage.

Error handling deficiencies often become apparent in production. Unexpected error conditions may not be properly caught and handled, error context may be insufficient for debugging, or error recovery may fail. Implementing comprehensive error handling with proper context capture helps diagnose these issues. Regular review of error logs helps identify patterns and systematic problems.

Dependency conflicts can create subtle issues in production. Package version mismatches between environments, system library incompatibilities, or conflicting package requirements can cause unexpected behavior. Using Docker containers helps ensure consistent environments. Regular dependency audits help identify potential conflicts before they impact production.

Performance bottlenecks may only become apparent under production loads. Database queries may perform poorly with larger datasets, algorithms may not scale as expected, or resource contention may impact throughput. Performance profiling under production like conditions helps identify these issues. Regular performance testing with production scale datasets helps catch potential problems during development.

Logging and monitoring gaps often hamper problem diagnosis in production. Log levels may be inappropriate, important metrics may be missing, or alert thresholds may be poorly tuned. Regular review of logging and monitoring effectiveness helps identify gaps. Implementing structured logging and proper context propagation helps with problem diagnosis.

Security vulnerabilities may be discovered in production. Authentication may be bypassed in unexpected ways, authorization may have gaps, or encryption may be insufficient. Regular security audits and penetration testing helps identify these issues. Implementing security monitoring and alerting helps detect potential attacks.

Data consistency issues can emerge in distributed systems. Race conditions during updates, partial failure during distributed transactions, or replication delays can create inconsistencies. Implementing proper consistency checks and reconciliation processes helps identify and resolve these issues. Regular data validation helps catch potential problems.

Integration points with external services often create production issues. API changes may break compatibility, rate limits may be exceeded, or service outages may impact functionality. Implementing proper API versioning and compatibility testing helps prevent these issues. Regular integration testing helps catch potential problems early.

Cache invalidation issues can impact application correctness. Cache entries may become stale, invalidation messages may be lost, or cache coherency may break down in distributed environments. Implementing proper cache monitoring and validation helps identify these issues. Regular cache effectiveness analysis helps optimize caching strategies.

State management problems often surface in distributed applications. Session state may be lost during failover, distributed locks may fail to release properly, or state synchronization may break down. Implementing proper state management patterns and monitoring helps prevent these issues. Regular testing of failover scenarios helps verify state handling.

Successful troubleshooting requires a systematic approach: gather relevant logs and metrics, reproduce the issue if possible, identify the root cause through careful analysis, implement and test a fix, and monitor to ensure the problem is resolved. Maintaining runbooks with common troubleshooting procedures helps teams respond effectively to production issues.

Regular review and updates of troubleshooting procedures helps teams maintain effectiveness as systems evolve. Building institutional knowledge through post mortems and documentation helps prevent recurring issues. Implementing automated testing for resolved issues helps prevent regressions.

Chapter 62: Future-Proofing Julia Applications

As we look toward building sustainable Julia applications that can stand the test of time, several key principles and practices emerge as essential for future proofing our code. The rapidly evolving nature of software development demands that we build systems that can adapt and scale as requirements change.

A foundational aspect of future proofing Julia applications is maintaining strict type discipline. While Julia's dynamic nature offers flexibility, leveraging the type system helps create more maintainable and adaptable code. Abstract types should be used to define interfaces, allowing concrete implementations to evolve independently. This approach enables new functionality to be added without breaking existing code paths.

Version compatibility requires careful attention when building long lived applications. Julia's package manager provides excellent tools for managing dependencies, but we must be thoughtful about which version ranges we specify. Being too restrictive with version bounds can make updates difficult, while being too permissive risks breaking changes. A balanced approach involves regularly testing against new package versions and maintaining comprehensive test coverage to catch compatibility issues early.

API design plays a crucial role in future proofing applications. Well designed APIs should be both intuitive and extensible. Multiple dispatch enables powerful extension patterns, allowing new functionality to be added without modifying existing code. Documentation should clearly specify the contract of each function, including type constraints and invariants that must be maintained.

Data serialization formats require special consideration for long term maintainability. While Julia's built in serialization is convenient, it can be fragile across versions. Using language agnostic formats like JSON, Protocol Buffers, or Apache Arrow provides better long term stability. When custom serialization is needed, version numbers should be embedded to enable format evolution.

Database schema design must account for future changes. Using migrations to manage schema evolution helps maintain data consistency as requirements change. Careful consideration should be given to column types and constraints to ensure they can accommodate future needs without requiring major restructuring.

Configuration management should be flexible enough to adapt to different deployment environments while maintaining security and manageability. Environment variables and configuration files should use clear naming conventions. Sensitive values should be handled through secure credential management systems that can evolve with security requirements.

Error handling patterns need to be robust and extensible. Custom error types should form a clear hierarchy that can accommodate new error conditions. Error messages should be informative while avoiding exposure of sensitive information. Logging should capture sufficient context for debugging while respecting privacy requirements.

Performance optimization strategies should focus on algorithmic efficiency and scalability rather than premature optimization. Code should be structured to allow performance critical sections to be identified and optimized independently. Benchmarking infrastructure should be maintained to track performance across versions.

Security considerations must adapt to evolving threats. Authentication and authorization systems should be modular to allow security measures to be enhanced or replaced. Cryptographic algorithms should be configured through parameters that can be updated as recommendations change. Regular security audits help identify areas needing improvement.

Monitoring and observability systems need to be comprehensive yet flexible. Metrics collection should use standardized interfaces that can adapt to different monitoring systems. Logging should be structured and include correlation IDs to enable distributed tracing. Alert thresholds should be configurable to adapt to changing requirements.

Testing strategies must evolve with the application. Unit tests should focus on behavior rather than implementation details. Integration tests should use interfaces that can accommodate changes in external services. Performance tests should verify scalability across different load patterns.

Deployment processes need to be automated and reproducible. Container images should be built from declarative specifications. Infrastructure as code should be used to manage deployment environments. Continuous integration pipelines should be maintainable and adaptable to new requirements.

Documentation requires ongoing attention to remain valuable. Architecture decisions should be recorded with context about the factors that influenced them. API documentation should be automatically generated from code while maintaining readable examples. Operational procedures should be regularly reviewed and updated.

Dependency management strategies should balance stability with the ability to adopt improvements. Direct dependencies should be carefully chosen and regularly updated. Transitive dependencies should be periodically audited for security issues and performance improvements.

Resource management patterns need to scale with usage. Connection pools should be configurable to handle different load patterns. Caching strategies should be adaptable to changing access patterns. Resource limits should be monitored and adjustable based on requirements.

State management approaches must be resilient to system evolution. Session handling should use formats that can be versioned. Distributed state should use protocols that can accommodate new consistency requirements. State migration tools should be maintained to handle format changes.

Integration patterns need to be flexible and maintainable. Service clients should use interfaces that can adapt to API changes. Message formats should include version information to enable format evolution. Integration tests should verify behavior across different versions.

By following these principles and regularly reviewing their effectiveness, we can build Julia applications that remain maintainable and adaptable as requirements evolve. Regular evaluation of emerging best practices and new language features helps ensure our applications can leverage improvements while maintaining stability.

Don't miss out!

Visit the website below and you can sign up to receive emails whenever Alexander Clifton publishes a new book. There's no charge and no obligation.

https://books2read.com/r/B-A-GVDVC-GPKIF

BOOKS 2 READ

Connecting independent readers to independent writers.

About the Publisher

Northwood Lore Books is an independent imprint dedicated to producing accessible, thought-provoking content through the use of advanced content generation systems. All books published under this imprint are created for educational or entertainment purposes only. Authors listed under this imprint use pen names and are not subject-matter experts. Accordingly, no material should be interpreted as financial, legal, medical, or professional advice. The information provided is general in nature, subject to change, and may not reflect the most current data or guidance. Readers are encouraged to consult official sources or qualified professionals before making decisions based on the content herein.

www.ingramcontent.com/pod-product-compliance
Lightning Source LLC
LaVergne TN
LVHW090317210926
848480LV00001B/278